52 People

Connecting with life through strangers

Jayson Krause

Driven By Passion Press.
ISBN: 0987848011
ISBN-13: 978-0-9878480-1-7

For Dallas

Stop Living with Strangers!

C Jay

TABLE OF CONTENTS

Prologue: Stranger 0 - Some other beginnings end.....**1**

Introduction: When strangers die.....**6**

Stranger 1: If they can't get close enough to hurt you.....**10**

Stranger 2: You can rejoice because thorns have roses.....**14**

Stranger 3: Free the child's potential.....**19**

Stranger 4: When you meet a man, you judge him by his clothes.....**22**

Stranger 5: For those who understand, no explanation is necessary.....**27**

Stranger 6: A haven in a heartless world.....**31**

Stranger 7: Help us make right what is wrong.....**36**

Stranger 8: Rising high against the wind.....**41**

Stranger 9: Beautiful things in the world cannot be seen or touched **45**

Stranger 10: Love makes all things easy.....**49**

Stranger 11: Sitting in a quiet room alone.....**53**

Stranger 12: The human mind is in chains.....**58**

Stranger 13: Energy in motion.....**63**

Stranger 14: When stars were just the holes to heaven.....**69**

Stranger 15: The greatest loss is what dies inside us as we live.....**73**

Stranger 16: People have the ability to build again.....**79**

Stranger 17: We don't stop playing because we grow old.....**83**

Stranger 18: Differences, definitions and similarities.....**88**

Stranger 19: The sunlight flashes off your windshield.....**93**

Stranger 20: What I might be.....**98**

Stranger 21: To be alive is to be vulnerable.....**102**

Stranger 22: Walk on the sun.....**108**

Stranger 23: Would you tell me, please.....**113**

Stranger 24: The best things in life are unexpected.....**117**

Stranger 25: The past is a foreign country…..**122**

Stranger 26: Make a new ending…..**126**

Stranger 27: I do not believe in failure…..**130**

Stranger 28: How does one become a butterfly?.....**134**

Stranger 29: Cherish her memory and let it live on…..**139**

Stranger 30: Will we be a big heal, or a great soul?.....**143**

Stranger 31: The Guy in the Glass…..**147**

Stranger 32: Our children teach us what life is all about…..**152**

Stranger 33: Utopia is only the shadow of a dream…..**157**

Stranger 34: Presence, recollection and anticipation …..**162**

Stranger 35: You are not meant for crawling…..**168**

Stranger 36: A baby is born with a need to be loved…..**172**

Stranger 37: Together we can do something wonderful…..**176**

Stranger 38: I would choose pain…..**180**

Stranger 39: Travel is more than the seeing of sights…..**184**

Stranger 40: If I'd just been myself…..**189**

Stranger 41: Once you've lost it you can never get it back…..**193**

Stranger 42: How high he bounces when he hits bottom…..**197**

Stranger 43: The way you see people is the way you treat them…..**201**

Stranger 44: The closest to being in control we will ever be…..**206**

Stranger 45: I'm not supposed to love you…..**210**

Stranger 46: Man, alone, can dream…..**214**

Stranger 47: Standing upon the shoulders of giants…..**219**

Stranger 48: On life's vast ocean diversely we sail…..**223**

Stranger 49: When I grow up…..**226**

Stranger 50: Time heals…..**230**

Stranger 51: I want to know…..**235**

Stranger 52: The final mystery…..**241**

Conclusion: Crusade for Meaningful Connection…..**247**

ACKNOWLEDGEMENTS

This journey would not have been possible without the support and encouragement of so many: I'd like to thank my wife Erin; her love, patience and undying support has been nothing short of amazing. My Father, Mother, Brother and Sister; who each have played important roles as counselor, editor, critic and cheering section. To my editor Heather Setka, who poured her heart into shaping and sculpting the project, and Kiah Gutowski for her copy-editing. Alec, who was a part of the brainstorm (along with Erin) that created this little idea. A heartfelt thank you to the many other friends who have given freely of their time and efforts, put forth ideas and encouraged me. Thank you to the Water Dragons – a special group of individuals who have supported me in so many ways. To Karen and Henry Kimsey-House and their creation: Co-Activity - this work has played a critical role in opening my eyes and my heart and calling forth the leader within me. Finally, I humbly thank the strangers who entered my life and allowed me to interview them.

NOTE TO THE READER:

The interviews with each stranger have been directly transcribed to provide you the most accurate experience of this journey. At times you may notice that question number ten (What question do you want me to ask you now?) has been omitted from the conversation. There were some interviews with which the question didn't elicit much of an answer - in these cases it has been left out of the book. Finally, all names of the strangers interviewed have been changed, with the exception of Dr. Demartini.

PROLOGUE
STRANGER 0

"Every beginning is some other beginning's end."
- Seneca

My phone was stuck in my pocket and I could feel it vibrate as I cruised down the highway just outside of Montreal. Fresh air flowed through my open window. One hand was on the steering wheel and the other was interlocked with my girlfriend's fingers as we headed to a fancy restaurant to cap off a long day trip to historic Quebec City.

It was early fall 2005 and I was staying with a friend in Montreal, a former Olympian and training specialist who I had planned to train with for two weeks in preparation for the upcoming Olympic season. My girlfriend at the time had flown out from her home in Toronto to visit for the weekend, and we spent a few wonderful days together. Life was going great, until I pulled my phone out and checked my voicemail.

My heart almost stopped as I listened to the voice of my best friend's wife tell me she didn't think Dallas, her husband, was going to make it through the night. I felt faint as the color instantly drained from my face. I hit the gas and frantically searched for the quickest route to the airport. My girlfriend became nervous and asked me what was going on. I couldn't speak. I had one thing on my mind: *Get to the airport.*

As we sped along the road, I struggled to explain the situation to her. But, she understood what was unfolding. She knew the story of Dallas and how he'd been in a battle with cancer for over 5 years. He had bounced between remission and relapse over several years and hadn't been doing so well when I left home a few days prior. His downward spiral began so quickly.

I had a brief conversation with Dallas the day before. He had called me to see how I was doing and how my training had been going. We exchanged some small talk about college football and the weather. Then I rushed him off the phone, almost as if he was an unwanted distraction at

1

the time. A tremendous wave of guilt overcame me as I wondered if the last conversation I would ever have with my best friend would be me giving him the brush off.

As I arrived at the airport, I left my girlfriend to park the car while I bolted inside. Finding the nearest ticket booth, I scrambled up to the front and pleaded with the woman standing there to find me the fastest ticket back home. My eyes swelled and the inside of my nose burned as I felt cool, salty tears run down my face and into my mouth. I waited as she clicked away at her computer. With dismay she finally responded, "I'm sorry sir, the last plane to Calgary left about thirty minutes ago."

I pleaded and begged for her to get me home as I explained the urgency of the situation. She frowned and looked at me with apologetic eyes, "The only thing I can do is get you on the first flight in the morning." My chest expanded and contracted quicker and quicker as intense anxiety kicked in. I felt trapped and helpless. Despite my emotions, I realized that fighting would be of no use, so I gave up and paid for the early morning ticket home.

The drive back to the house in Montreal was quiet and painful. A million scenarios raced through my head as I pleaded with the sky, the universe, anybody, or anything to help me. I prayed that if there was a god, to please, please let me get home to say goodbye to my friend. The night was long.

I arrived at the airport early and then spent the entire four-hour flight in a complete daze. I had so much going through my mind but I couldn't focus enough to write in my journal, talk, watch a movie, or sleep. The flight felt painfully slow.

As soon as I landed, my brother was there to greet me with a big hug. He seemed calm and relaxed. He explained the current situation and how Dallas had seemed to regain stability. Hearing my brother's reassuring story settled my nerves and had me feeling better. Despite the positive news, we still rushed out to the car and were quickly en-route to the hospital. We arrived just before noon and my heart was full of joy after hearing Dallas was OK. My prayers were answered. In fact, they were exceeded. He was going to be OK.

The elevator dinged and slowly opened. Then I nervously approached the hospital room door to peek inside. I was not prepared for what appeared before me. The hope my brother had provided was instantly shattered as I stood in complete fear gazing at what appeared to be the shell of my best friend sitting on the edge of his bed. He was gesturing wildly to his wife, Jennifer. Struggling and virtually incoherent, he pushed away her attempts to assist him and unsuccessfully tried to communicate something. I was scared. Completely paralyzed with fear, I didn't know what to do.

Surely as white as a ghost, I walked slowly into the room. I believed I was witnessing the moment of his death. The truth of the moment was that Dallas was so incredibly drugged up that he couldn't communicate and was delirious. He was speaking gibberish that nobody could interpret. Once the doctor turned the painkilling drugs down, Dallas began to regain his composure. Much to my surprise, a few hours passed and he was almost his old self again. There we were, back to small talk about football, my trip to Montreal, bugging his wife…it was going to be OK.

It had been a roller coaster of emotions, but it seemed as though the ride had come to a stop and Dallas appeared to be on the path towards recovery. Once he fell asleep and I was confident with his recovery, I slipped out and went home to shower and change my clothes before returning to watch the Monday night football game with him.

When I arrived back early that evening, Dallas was bouncing back and forth between sleep and consciousness. We had 15 minute snippets of conversations here and there. He would comment on the game and then quickly fall back asleep. This repeated over and over many times.

There were three of us hanging out with Dallas on that night: myself; another high school friend, Pablo; and Jennifer. We talked while we all sat at his side and watched the game.

Dallas seemed to be struggling to breathe as the night wore on. The plastic mask firmly attached to his face pumped concentrated oxygen into his body. But, I noticed as the night went on his neck muscles would increasingly contract with more intensity. Every contraction jolted his body slightly upward as the hiss and pop of the machine forced his lungs to work. He was fighting.

The football game ended. I walked out into the hall to stretch my legs when I was quickly called back into the room. Dallas was awake and sitting up. He motioned with his hands that he wanted to say something. His wife sat cross-legged on the bed staring at him. He was back into a deeply drugged state. He swung his head back and forth as he struggled to say something to us. His hands moved rapidly as if communicating through a game of charades, but none of us knew what he was trying to say. I rubbed his back and his wife rubbed his legs as he bobbled back and forth, staring into her eyes. She then held his head. Almost touching nose to nose, she repeated over and over with a soft sweet voice, "I love you Dall, I love you, I love you…"

Overcome with emotion, Jennifer left the room momentarily and Dallas swung his head over and stared at me. Our eyes locked and memories of our childhood escapades flooded in. The vibrant, mischievous lad who used to cause trouble with me, who supported me, and who I loved dearly now wavered. I winked at him and through his glazed eyes and stoic face I could see his eyes light up. That moment will remain etched in my memory forever.

Jennifer returned and the four of us sat together: Jennifer lying beside him on the bed holding him and Pablo and me at his side. We were all sitting quietly, yet Dallas sat up with urgency and started shushing us. He removed the tightly fitting mask that had been a fixture on his face the entire day and he fought to speak. Complete focus and all his effort went into timing his breath as he looked up and forced out some words.

"If you're… happy… and you know it… clap your hands…"

The only words that came out of his mouth in hours made us all smile. We continued the song he had started, singing happily in unified chorus as he retreated back into the semi-horizontal position on the bed, put his mask back on, and leaned back watching us with delight as we sang on.

The song ended and we all sat there relishing in the beauty of the moment and the miraculous strength Dallas had conjured up to sing. It was beautiful and yet my heart ached. Tears rolled down my face.

This man is incredible.

There was a long silence.

The machine no longer hissed and popped and the muscles on his neck no longer contracted... his song had been sung and he had sailed away.

INTRODUCTION
WHEN STRANGERS DIE

"That's what makes deaths so hard - unsatisfied curiosity."
- Beryl Marcham

My best friend died a stranger to me.

I was the best man at his wedding and gave the eulogy at his funeral. He had lost a long battle with cancer and I was at his side for the struggle between remission and relapse before he passed away. Yet, the stinging pain of his death was the brutal realization that after spending so much time together over fifteen years I knew very little about who he really was.

We did what most people do with their time together, we stuck to the surface of our conversations. We spent over fifteen years talking about football, sharing drunken stories, and reveling in tales of collective mischief. Everything we spoke about were frivolous external things, nothing about our internal experiences. During his sickness, I felt it was my job as his best friend to shelter him and myself from the reality of his condition. I thought we could coast along happily avoiding any conversation that might lead to even greater emotional discomfort. Of course, all of this led to feelings of anger, guilt, and painful regret once he passed away. But, I didn't know what all of this pain was until it struck me one day. He died a stranger to me. I never *really* knew him. How many other strangers are there in my life? The hard answer: everyone.

Most people don't know the real me: the emotions, fears, and dreams behind the omnipresent confident façade. I wanted to truly get to know the people in my life. Could that be so hard?

We spend so much time with the people in our lives, but for some reason rarely stop to actually listen to what they want from life and what drives their anger or sadness. To complicate things, texting, BBM, and social networking tools have made the phone call or face-to-face conversation obsolete. People have become socially lazy. Relationships now, even more so than before, tend to be built and sustained on the feeble foundations of whatever can be expressed within 140 characters or less.

About 18 months after Dallas' death, on the morning of my realization, I felt I had to do something about it. This is when 52 People was born.

52 People was going to be an experiment, a challenge, and a dedication to my late friend Dallas. It was to be a demonstration that could inspire people to look at their own lives and develop meaningful relationships with the strangers around them, especially those living under the same roof.

The premise of 52 People is as follows: In a world of electronic relationships, how willing will someone be to sit down with a complete stranger (me) face-to-face and answer 10 insightful questions about themselves?

The more I looked, the more I realized I was surrounded by strangers in my life. That was until I started researching and developing this experiment. I had no idea – concerning the depth of my parents, siblings, and friends – what made them truly tick. The rewards of this experiment arose instantly when I began testing the questions on my family members. Escaping from the hum-drum of canned conversation about the weather, sports, extended family issues and pop culture we instead immersed ourselves in rich dialogue concerning who they were as people. This immediately became a priceless experience.

I sat down alone with each of my family members. After 31 years on the planet, I then witnessed my family as completely different people. My Dad spent the whole time in tears, wiping his eyes after every single answer. The man, who in my eyes epitomized strong work ethic, uttered the words "this is so hard." My brother apologized for breaking down into tears when speaking about his children. My mother stopped her busy-bodying and quietly and thoughtfully opened up her heart and let me peek in. My sister, who normally is elusive in her expression and articulation, poured out her dreams, fears, and wisdom. In such a short time of meaningful expression, my family lost their labels as simply Mom, Dad,

Brother, and Sister and became completely different people. After this initial test, I knew I was on to something.

The Format:

Beginning on my 32nd birthday (January 8th, 2009), everywhere I went I took with me a small digital recorder. Each week I approached a complete stranger in attempt to invite them to answer 10 personal questions. If I was rejected, I would keep on going until I found someone willing to connect. I targeted a variety of locations to provide a large cross-section of individuals. Each "stranger" represented a week in the following year of adventures in rejection and connection. My intentions were to connect with 52 complete strangers and inspire them to connect with the people in their lives: to ask the questions and have meaningful conversations with their loved ones. Also along this journey, there were a few myths I set out to debunk about real connection:

Connection with others is difficult - It takes too much time.
People will think I'm weird by approaching them to connect.
Most people will reject me.
People will not be open with me.
People do not want to connect, they want to be left alone.
People have enough meaningful connection already in their lives.

The Questions:

I began with about 50 questions and whittled them down by asking friends and family members. I chose the final questions based on what evoked the strongest answers. If people responded by saying, "That one's really hard", then I knew I had a good one. The questions I chose were simple, yet they forced the individuals to look deep inside, quite often, to places they have wandered far from or have never visited before.

Once I had the questions, I arranged them in a way that wouldn't have people running away after the first one came out of my mouth. I specifically designed the flow of the questions so that they began with possibility and creativity and built to a more 'uncomfortable' crescendo.

Part way through the experiment another question peeked out at me and I couldn't refuse it as it added an interesting touch to the conversation.

1. If you could create your dream job what would it be?

2. What fulfills you?

3. What is your greatest fear?

4. What do you want more of in your life?

5 a) What is your greatest accomplishment?

5 b) What are you most ashamed of? (added part way through the experiment)

6. What makes you sad?

7. What is the most difficult thing you've ever experienced?

8. What is great about you?

9. Who are you?

10. What question do you want me to ask you now?

I had my questions, my digital recorder, and a deep igniting reason for the experiment. All I needed next was my first stranger.

STRANGER 1

"If they can't get close enough to hurt you, they can't get close enough to love you."
- Anonymous

She spends her days walking and contemplating. She spends her days surrounded by a pack. She spends her days both yearning for and fearing the weapon of love.

It was my 32nd birthday and the first day of 52 People. I woke up with a fresh feeling of new beginnings, or perhaps it was nervous energy about the looming encounters and strangers who were somewhere out there in the world awaiting my questions.

Nervousness, excitement, and uncertainty filled my body while I searched for stranger number one. I had my questions in my pocket along with my digital voice recorder. All I needed to do was engage the first stranger and begin the long awaited adventure. My chosen venue to start the whole thing off was the dog park. I picked a time, mid morning, when I figured there wouldn't be many people out and I might cross paths with a solitary dog walker.

Anxious yet excited, I gripped the steering wheel tightly as my car slowly rolled to a stop, while my dog Ruthie yelped with joy. There was much less activity than I'd hoped for; the park was seemingly empty. Even my dog looked disappointed as she scanned the empty field in search of a playmate. But, just when I thought I'd have to develop an alternative plan, we were unexpectedly greeted by Stranger 1. Stranger 1 was somewhere in her mid-to-late thirties and she had long dark hair that ran down the back of her winter coat. I joined her and the eight dogs that formed her pack and we all walked together for quite a while, most of which I conversed with myself inside my head.

Ask her.... do it now, I repeated inside my head over and over.

It was like I was in junior high school and I desperately wanted to ask a girl to dance but the nerves had me frozen. Instead, we walked in silence mostly as we watched the dogs wrestle and chase each other in the deep snow.

My internal struggle lasted for quite some time before I finally broke the silence by loudly blurting, "I have a question for you!"

Seriously? That's what I just said? Oh no, she's going to freak out and call her dogs over here to protect her.

Much to my surprise, she looked over at me politely and curiously as I attempted to recover by explaining my experiment. Then I made my sales pitch. I sensed a bit of hesitation, but she agreed. The experiment officially began.

1) What is your dream job?

"I'm already doing it – A dog walker. And, I would like to do more with it – more animal communication and working with horses, working with animals in a healing capacity. Animals are more in touch with the source and they are unconditional right? Just to be more in tune with that. I just merge with that energy."

2) What fulfills you?

"Merging with the other side. Earth is very 3D – limited – you get people and politics and stuff like that. Merging more with the source I suppose. I'm a very idealistic person so it would be nice to be merging more with that - the better side of people. So, for me – if you want to talk about the god or whatever, but that bliss over on the other side – that satisfies me a great deal when I can get in tune with that."

3) What is your greatest fear?

"Love… being hurt by love."

4) What do you want more of in your life?

"I could do with a bit more money to finish fixing up my house, pay off some debt and share it with some friends who need it."

5) What is the greatest accomplishment of your life?

"I think my life. I have had a very interesting life. How I've developed myself – I'm pretty proud of that. I've taken risks. I've done a lot of things, unconventional things, and I think at the end of the day from where I started to where I am now I've done a good job."

6) What makes you sad?

"Seeing people or animals in pain. The injustices in the world. That pains me a great deal. I can watch a commercial and cry. I'd like to see a bit more compassion."

7) What is the most difficult thing you've ever experienced?
"My mother's death."

8) What is great about you?
"I have a real sense of compassion. I have a great deal of compassion. I'm very bright, but that's not important – that's just my brain. I have a real sense of lovingness and gentleness that I think is kind of unique. I'm more of a spiritual person, so a lot of the physical stuff doesn't matter to me."

9) Who are you?
"I think I'm just here on this planet to kind of help people bring some light into this world and learn my own lessons. I'm just trying to make this world a better place. So, I think that's my focus."

Stranger one's greatest fear is being hurt by love. I could feel the pain in her quiet, trembling voice as it softened while she uttered, "…being hurt by love." Many people, myself included, have been hurt by love in some way throughout our lives and can empathize with those painful feelings.

Love can be a scary place. When we open ourselves up to someone and fully expose our dreams and intentions, it can feel like standing blindfolded on the edge of a cliff. We don't know if the object of our affection will push us off the edge, turn around and walk away, or join us on the edge of vulnerability. To prevent the pain of rejection we often recede back to the safety of sure, stable ground while still yearning to go back to the edge. But we don't. Yet, the edge is the place where we truly develop loving, meaningful relationships – the place of vulnerability and trust. The edge is the beautiful place we both fear and long for – where two people, hand in hand count to three and jump off together.

Today, I stepped to my edge with a complete stranger. I didn't know how she would respond, or how the interview would end up. The stories I made up in my mind before beginning the conversation were fearful tales of her screaming at me for asking an offensive question and telling me to get far away from her. The reality was exactly the opposite. Today I stepped to the edge by beginning something that feels both important to me and scares me. This is the edge that I want to stand on over the next year as I approach people in my life each week. My hope in doing this is to make standing on the edge with people become easier. As I come to the edge with complete strangers and step to the edge with the people closest to me, I realize I may get hurt, but I also realize I may experience more meaningful connection. There's only one way to find out.

STRANGER 2

*"You can complain because roses have thorns,
or you can rejoice because thorns have roses."*
- Ziggy

*He may not have what we have, but he has something else – something
great. This thing allows him to do what most of us would conceive as
unimaginable.*

I kissed my wife, Erin, goodbye and she walked through the security gates
to board a plane heading for Frankfurt, Germany. As she disappeared
through the doors, my intention quickly turned towards engaging a second
stranger. As I wandered about the airport, I was dismayed at how empty it
appeared. The airport was a place where I thought finding a solo stranger
would be like picking apples from a ripe orchard.

Like a slow moving boat, I trolled the area until I spotted a young,
sharply dressed man reading a book. Not nearly as awkward as last week, I
eloquently attempted to engage his company. "Sorry, I've got to leave in
five minutes, but it sounds interesting," he explained.

There it is, my first rejection – not *nearly as harrowing as I had*
anticipated.

Actually, I felt relieved to get the first official rejection out of the
way. I knew there would be more, but to face the rejection and keep
moving was a small victory.

I walked the length of the airport and amongst the smattering of
people I was unable to find anyone sitting alone. I was just about to pack
up and consider another venue until I spotted a man who caught my eye, so
I approached him to become stranger number two. I didn't have to do
much selling as he enthusiastically agreed to sit down and answer my
questions.

Stranger 2 was a 29-year-old airline ambassador, ranch hand, and
War Amps consultant – who was born with no arms and no legs.

1) What is your dream job?

"It would involve a lot of traveling and a lot of interaction with people. There is this travel show idea another friend and I have. I'd love to get paid to travel the different places of the world, do neat activities, and meet all kinds of people. With traveling it's neat just to meet people and visit with people and see the world. If I could get paid to do that – Great! Perfect!"

2) What fulfills you?

"I have a lot of interests and a lot of passions and even when I think I've figured out what they all are I come across something else where I think 'holy crap' that's neat. I love people. I love the interaction. Being outdoors, I love being outside – fresh air and experiencing stuff. Pushing myself. When I'm not here, I work with my brother on a ranch and I'll jump on a tractor for a few hours. Or, if we're digging trenches for underground wires I'll grab a shovel and I'll dig two feet under for a ten foot long trench. I'll do all those kind of things, and I like doing those kind of things because most people would think 'He wouldn't be able to do that,' then I do it. I like pushing myself, traveling, sports. I snowboard, ski, and golf. Those things fulfill me – I guess in all of that – accomplishing something that a lot of people might not see someone like myself accomplishing."

3) What is your greatest fear?

"I don't want to live life and just be another blip on the radar screen. I want to be somebody who made a difference – who people looked up too and fed off of. When I accomplish something, I want to go further. I don't want to just do something. If I do something people say, 'oh that's cute, a little a guy with no arms and no legs tried surfing.' No, I want to go surfing and do it well so people can say, 'Wow that guys good!'"

4) What do you want more of in your life?

"To see more. I've seen a lot, but I want to see more of the world, meet more people, and get more experiences under my belt. I mean, I don't want to go running with the bulls – I don't have a death wish – just more experiences."

5) What is the greatest accomplishment of your life?

"This last trip to Brazil. In the sixth grade, we did a project in Brazil and (had) always wanted to go. I swam in the Amazon River, went piranha fishing, and surfing."

"I guess doing the snowboard thing, golfing, those are all things. Just getting myself to the point where I am now – just as a whole – and just continue building that."

6) What makes you sad?

"I'm a sucker for other people being upset. I hate seeing other people suffer. I'm always wanting to help them laugh or cheer them up in some way. I'm more than happy to sit down and talk with people and listen for a few hours. People will say, 'oh you're the last person I should be complaining to.' But, everybody has their down days. You're allowed to feel sorry for yourself. I don't care if you're griping to someone who has no arms and no legs. If you're having a shitty day, you're having a shitty day. Gripe!"

7) What is the most difficult thing you have ever experienced?

"I've had a pretty easy life in the grand scheme of things. The worst thing was when my five-year-old cousin passed away from cancer, and two months later another one of my cousins. She was three and in a wind storm that blew over a tree and it landed on her and killed her. Two funerals where the coffin wasn't big enough to have six pallbearers; somebody that young isn't supposed to be dying. There is no justifiable reason why a three-year-old girl who never had an opportunity to do wrong in her life has had her life cut short. Then you see bad people doing bad things and it seems like they live to be ninety-five-years-old and they never seem to get anything as bad as a cold."

8) What is great about you?

"I'm a very humble person. When people tell me I'm inspiring, I never know what to say. I guess I always try and make sure I have a smile on my face. I'm a very positive person and I'm always in the mood to laugh and joke around and have fun. Even on my bad days I can still manage to have a good day."

9) Who are you?

"Just a person that likes to have fun. Just a person who likes new experiences, meeting people. When you see me, I'm a guy that has no arms and no legs but it seems a lot worse than it actually is. That's me."

10) What question do you want me to ask you now?

"You've just asked me nine questions and now you want me to ask you to ask me one more? Ask me who the ideal companion is."

Who is the ideal companion?

"The ideal companion for me is not too tall – if you want to get into the physical stuff – cause I'm only four feet tall when I stand on my legs. The ideal companion is someone who enjoys life, has a good sense of humor, someone also likes to travel, someone not very caught up in the material part of life."

What do we choose to see in each moment of our lives? I was taken aback when Stranger 2 made the statement that he has had a "pretty easy life in the grand scheme of things." Pretty easy life? I'm sure there are many people out there with all four limbs and complete health who consider their lives to be one monumental struggle after another. Nothing goes right for these people because the cloud is always over their heads and the rain never stops. They can never get ahead, or some oppressive regime makes it impossible for them to enjoy life. Do you know people like this?

It boils down to perception – the perceptions we carry about our lives.

My hairline seems to be rapidly receding with each passing day. Shall I stare into the mirror and curse old age sneaking up on me, or shall I embrace the wisdom that accompanies each year of experience? I spent close to twelve years training to compete at the Olympics. Should I dwell in the failures and disappointments of not reaching them, or do I bask in the valuable lessons, experiences and opportunities that have arisen from the journey?

We all have experienced "thorns" at some point in our lives. We can choose to focus our energy on the thorns, allowing ourselves to get caught up in the painful sting delivered by each sharp point, or you can focus on the intricate beauty of the rose that lies at the top of each sharp stem. Rejoice because every thorn is like a rung on a ladder that leads to captivating beauty and a powerful sweet scent that clings to your soul as you travel through life.

I started my day with rejection – a thorn. I could have easily skulked away with the stinging pain of rejection as I have at times in my past. Today I stuck around long enough to be able to witness the rose awaiting me. The rejection was exactly what I needed to push me in the direction of the treasures of wisdom offered by Stranger 2.

How important is choosing a powerful perspective at any given moment? When Stranger 2 and I sat down I would have never guessed I was sitting with a surfer, snowboarder, and adventure traveler. At the end of our conversation, the man born with no arms and no legs stood up and walked back to work.

STRANGER 3

"Free the child's potential and you will transform him into the world."
- Maria Montessori

Standing in front of his pupils, he waits to witness what the result of his actions will be. Wait for it. Wait for it. There it is.

A few condiments sat bunched together – the last remnants of what was at one time a fridge rife with a variety of fresh foods. I stood peering inside, hoping to find a few complimentary pieces of food that might combine to make something edible. Lacking success, I conceded and went to the grocery store in search of something to fill my desperately hungry belly.

The fact I chose the grocery store over a fast food joint was a success in itself as normally my default would be to swing open the double doors of the burger joint across the street and wait for the staff to stop what they were doing and greet me by my first name.

Before I started tossing items into my grocery basket, I figured I'd take a stroll around to see if there were any solo shoppers who could be prospective strangers. My attention was caught by a long line of people standing in the hallway outside the produce section. Curious to see what the commotion was about, I decided to explore further. As I rounded the corner, the flashing blue screen jumped out at me. "Lotto jackpot - 43 Million Dollars!" The allure of financial freedom sucked me in as I joined the congregation of dream seekers. I took my place in line, observing the wide-eyed people around me. All of us looked entranced by the thought of holding the winning numbers.

Standing directly in front of me was Stranger number three. Like a jungle cat stalking his prey, I formulated the plan inside my head. As he paid for his ticket and turned to leave, I pounced. At first, I wasn't sure I was going to get him, but I made the pitch and he cautiously agreed.

Stranger number three was a grey haired high school teacher, father and husband – who we'll call Mr. Keating.

1) What is your dream job?

"My dream job at this time would be probably some sort of travel consultant where I'd have to travel to a lot of different countries and experience a lot of different cultures."

2) What fulfills you?

"I'm a teacher and that's part of what fulfills me; and so I enjoy my job, and my family and friends and that kind of stuff. What we call the 'ah ha!' moment when kids are learning something that you're trying to teach."

3) What is your greatest fear?

"I would say that people will find out that I haven't reached my fullest potential."

4) What do you want more of in your life?

"Time to travel – time and money to travel."

5) What is the greatest accomplishment of your life?

"My family."

6) What makes you sad?

"More melancholy than sad – a bad day of work can. Things with my family. Nothing in particular sticks out as making me really sad. I would get upset by stuff like that, but sad is more – again the way I interpret it – is more personal. Nothing in particular, I can't say anything gets me. No, I'm a fairly easy going guy."

7) What is the most difficult thing you've ever experienced?

"Boy, you've got tough questions here. I haven't had to think of this stuff for a lot of years. Nothing comes to mind immediately. One of my children went through some very difficult times at one part of her life, which had an impact on the whole family. So, that's what comes to mind right now. I would say that, or any difficulties that my children have encountered – certainly for the last, soon to be, 30 years of my life. That's probably what comes to mind."

8) What is great about you?

"I'm a good person and a good father – I guess is what I'd consider to be great about me."

9) Who are you?

"I'll come back to the same thing. I'm a father, a husband, a teacher – in terms of who I see myself and things I'm comfortable with. I'm a good easy going human being who just, more or less, likes life."

Mr. Keating is in the "potential" business. He devotes each day to developing the potential of his students: engaging the students in discussion, demonstrating a lesson, or creatively revealing the path to realization. Mr. Keating is the custodian for knowledge, a conduit for producing the "Ah Ha!" moment of realization in their minds. While he spends his days luring the potential out of his pupils, his worst fear is having others realize he hasn't reached his own potential.

I'll tell you what Mr. Keating – I hope I never realize my potential.

The word potential assumes that there is a destination. What if you reach your "potential" when you are young? Does that make your job complete? Do you sit back and wait to die as you have done all you can do? When potential is freed, then opportunity awaits. It is here that we realize there are only progress and growth and no destination to be measured. Actualizing potential every day is looking back and asking yourself: am I better today than I was yesterday?

Mr. Keating was passionate about creating the "Ah Ha!" moment experienced by his students. But Mr. Keating, *I just have one more question for you?*

Mr. Keating, O Captain, my Captain...who does this for you?

You are a not only a husband, father, and teacher, but a life-long student with never ending potential. Remove the barriers, stretch yourself, free your potential and let yourself grow and you will be transformed into the world.

STRANGER 4

"When you meet a man, you judge him by his clothes; when you leave, you judge him by his heart."
- Russian proverb

Cash once flowed into his hands like water from a fountain, now he is penniless. At 49 years old, he fears he may not live to celebrate his fiftieth birthday.

I had no plan other than to catch the city train and go where the tracks would take me in search of the next stranger. Several people clambered on and off of the train, making it unusually busy for a Saturday afternoon. I rode as far as downtown, where I disembarked and walked towards a busy street. I approached one woman sitting alone, but due to her lack of proficiency in English she didn't feel comfortable answering my questions. Another older woman also thwarted my attempts. "Sounds nice, but I'm not interested," she said. I was now beginning to get used to the rejection. As I approached each stranger, I would often say to myself, *Shoot for no.* That way I wouldn't be disappointed if they rejected my offer.

Continuing to search, I rounded the corner of a building and almost stumbled over a shopping cart full of what appeared to be garbage. Nearby, a man stood bent over, head buried deep into a garbage can. He emerged from the can, turned around, and looked in my direction as if he was expecting me. He shook the garbage off of a coffee cup and explained, "There is a cigarette butt in it, but this will work."

"What are you going to do with that?" I asked him

Motioning towards McDonalds, he sheepishly smiled, "Going to claim my refill."

Acting like an embarrassed host, he quickly pointed to a bag he cradled in his free arm.

"Want a cookie?" he asked.

"No thank you," I graciously replied.

He sported a felt lined denim storm rider jacket and a thick sailor's beanie sat on top of his head. A scraggly pointed white beard grew like weeds from his face – no doubt keeping him warm during the cold winter. He motioned over to a nearby bench and invited me to sit down with him. I accepted his kind request and we were soon chatting like old friends.

I explained *52 people* to him and he immediately became interested. He offered his advice on the experiment, "Depending on how you use it, this could be very valuable information."

This was one of the times where the cold steel of the train tracks on Saturday afternoon transported me to the perfect place: the waiting hands of Lenny.

1) What is your dream job?

"My dream job is to actually return to where I was and go back to doing what I was doing almost ten years ago: teaching English in Taiwan. This was the dream job of a lifetime. I went there in February of 1980 to get off the streets and away from drugs and away from bad influences. I fortunately had parents who may not have had the financial means but they had the motivation and they cared enough about me that they found a way. Their original plan was to get me off the streets and away from the downward spiral I was on."

2) What fulfills you?

"Helping people. I remember that when I first started teaching English, the first thing I noticed, what I really liked about it, was that I wasn't thinking about when class was over and I wasn't thinking about how much money I was making or when I was gonna get paid. I enjoyed it so much I didn't want class to end. I didn't want my students to leave. But, of course – like every good thing – sooner or later it has to come to an end."

3) What is your greatest fear?

"Either getting robbed and possibly beaten to death or dying from a drug overdose. I've had close to eight or nine O.D.s in the last twelve months."

4) What do you want more of in your life?

"Contact with people, and the opportunity to teach English again."

5) What is the greatest accomplishment of your life?

"Probably, successfully teaching about five thousand people in Taiwan."

6) What makes you sad?

"The thought that I'll never get back to what I was originally doing. The thought that I'll never teach again. The thought that I'll never see the Orient again."

7) What is the most difficult thing you've ever experienced?

"Getting through neck surgery after having my neck broken. A teenager saw me and his friend fighting. I tried to run and ran off the curb and fell flat on my face. I was just trying to get up when he got right up behind me and kicked me in the back of the head – just like a football player would kick a football trying to make a field goal except for the fact that my head was connected to my body and instead of flying through the air it snapped my neck and crushed the uppermost two vertebrae. Wearing a halo for 4 months (you can still see the divots in my head). Wearing the halo was extremely irritating, if not painful."

8) What is great about you?

"The greatest thing about me, I think, is my ability to adapt."

9) Who are you?

"I was taught at a very young age by my father how to sell. (I'm) A good salesman – one of the top ten most successful teachers in Taiwan at the time I was there. I would also consider myself an excellent father. I spent most of the time necessary to raise my three sons, while my wife in turn spent most of her time teaching and preparing material."

10) What question do you want to ask me now?

"This is a good question, but I don't know if I can answer it. The question is how do I plan on getting out of the position that I'm in right now?"

How do you plan on getting out of the position you are in now?

"Persistence, planning, devotion, what you might call abstract or lateral thinking. I try not to look at other people's position and how they got out of their mess. I basically have to do what I did before, only without my parent's help."

I am guilty of judging a man by his clothes.

Never did I expect to have the depth of conversation that I shared with Lenny. For some reason, I assumed he would provide much different answers from what an "average" person would have. I had never talked to a homeless person before. I had no idea what to expect. All I had were my assumptions about the homeless. Lenny taught me about judgment.

We talked for over an hour about various issues: meaningful relationships, traveling, the economy, crime, you name it. He told me of his addiction to morphine and his inability to escape from it. He spoke of the need to numb his physical pain and openly spoke about the pain from past memories.

When our visit came to an end we held a strong handshake and Lenny looked through my eyes deep into my core. "I believe that people meet each other for a reason," he said, as our hands parted. "I believe in that kind of destiny stuff."

The cold wind that day had indeed blown me to the right spot. I had judged him by the clothes on his back when we first met, but the expansiveness of his heart quickly erased the preconceived notions I'd held. My assumptions were completely wrong. Assumptions create barriers and prevent us from truly opening up to one another and experiencing the real side of people. My assumptions almost robbed me of a rich connection.

Later that evening, I told someone about my interview with Lenny.

"So did you buy him a coffee?" he asked.

I sat there stunned when it hit me that I didn't. I felt ashamed. Why didn't I at least buy him a coffee?

Shortly before I had met Lenny, I enjoyed a five dollar truffle espresso in the warmth and coziness of a Starbucks. A few minute later, I was watching him shake a cigarette butt from an old cup so he could get a coffee of his own. I spent over an hour with a guy who was just searching for a way to get a warm drink by digging through the trash, and I didn't even buy him a coffee.

The big lesson and truth to the situation was simple. After sitting with him, I judged him by his heart instead of his appearance. I had made a friend. I walked away and had completely forgotten he was a homeless man.

STRANGER 5

"For those who understand, no explanation is necessary... for those who do not, none is possible."
- George Seaton

She sits and waits for it to come. Looking out in the distance she can sense it coming. It gets bigger and seems to pick up velocity as it blasts closer. At the perfect time, she begins to paddle as hard as she can. Jumping up, she balances as the wave shoots her towards the shore.

I fought through the crowd as people walked clustered, shoulder-to-shoulder, over Charles Bridge in Prague, Czech Republic. It was just over 10 minutes until the new year was to be ushered in. I was going against the grain as I walked from the centre of the city in search of higher ground I had made little progress since the crowd had slowed to a standstill. People all around me anticipated the countdown and had begun early celebrations. The excitement built and the volume increased into a deafening roar as people sang, hollered, and threw firecrackers into the air. Fireworks lit up the night sky as couples kissed, friends hugged, and the energy of new beginnings reflected off the faces of many around me. 2005 had now arrived. Amidst millions of people in one of the most beautiful places in the world, I had never before felt so completely alone.

Why am I sharing this story with you? Because my conversation with Stranger number 5 conjured up those memories of feeling alone.

My weekend was spent assisting in a weekend course educating aspiring life coaches. My lunch break was the best time for me to find the next stranger and I spotted her as I walked up the steps from the basement board room. She stood there alone, looking slightly unsure of what she was doing or where she was going, and I felt the urge to approach and enroll her in my experiment. Lucky for me, she had the time and willingness to do it.

Stranger number 5 was a young corporate woman who is beautiful, successful and lonely – a twin separated by thousands of miles from the rest of her family.

1) What is your dream job?

"Having a little dive shop off the coast of an ocean – scuba diving. I feel free when I'm 60 feet under. If I could do that for a living and if I was just diving with people all the time or seeing them do it for the first time, yeah that would be my dream job – with a little tiki bar on the side."

2) What fulfills you?

"That is a question that I'm still trying to answer."

3) What is your greatest fear?

"Being alone – just not having that constant support – Being alone in the sense of not having a life partner, or like, a significant other. It's when you ask, that I think of all the celebrations I've had in my life, or everything I achieve, and everywhere I go and I turn around and want to tell somebody and they're not there. So, that's the way it is now, and I'm afraid it's going to be like that for a very long time."

4) What do you want more of in your life?

"Balance. My life seems like it's all over the place right now. Between work, stress, money, career, family, all these big choices that I have to make, I'm in that time where I have to make these choices because that will change the direction my life is going right now. Yeah, I just feel like I'm all over the place and I need to find that calm."

5 a) What is your greatest accomplishment?

"I think for me it's a combination of some things that I've done. There's been a lot of things that people have told me that I couldn't do and I proved them wrong. So, I did it and that was a sense of accomplishment to me: when I went to university, when I traveled around the world, the job that I'm in now."

This is where I began adding the question: What are you most ashamed of?

5 b) What are you most ashamed of?

"Ashamed of? Oh. Personality wise? I look younger than I am so I find that people don't take me seriously so sometimes I'm ashamed of how overboard I can get just to prove my point because of that."

6) What makes you sad?

"Being away from my family and friends. They are just not physically here. I moved across the country. Friends are scattered and family is still there."

7) What is the most difficult thing you've experienced?

"This is going to make me cry – my sister trying to commit suicide. She is my twin sister. So, worst time of my life."

8)What is great about you?

"Well I don't know!"

"I'm not judgmental, I guess. It falls under not being judgmental – I like seeing the differences in people and I'm pretty open about that."

9) Who are you?

"I think in a sense I'm still trying to figure that one out too. Like, I know what some of my beliefs are, or where my values and everything lie, or who I want to be. I'm not sure if it's that person yet though. Does that make sense? I'm like a wave, it's coming in and then it goes right back out."

10) What question do you want me to ask you now?

"I could give you a question, but I wouldn't be able to answer it, because I don't know the answer. But, I can think about it…What will make me happy?"

What will make you happy?

"I don't know yet. I guess, not really happy, fulfilled. You asked me a question earlier about that, so something to think about. But, I don't know if I can answer it."

––––––––––

When I was in Prague, I was searching for something – Love, connection, meaning, I don't know, but I strongly desired to have something. My heart was drenched with a sorrow I can't explain. Maybe the only way to label the pain is to call it loneliness. There is nothing I wanted more in the world than to have someone standing next to me as I scanned the explosion of colour overtop the Prague skyline. Imagining myself in love walking with a beautiful woman clinging tightly to my arm was what my heart wanted more than anything else. As I walked through the city, I would make eye contact with a pretty young lady in hopes of sparking up a stunning conversation. It never happened. I watched a young couple glued together, standing along the rail of the bridge, tossing chunks of bread to a flock of crazy sea gulls. I watched with jealousy as my mind created taunting images of myself in the same situation.

Over the years, I had spent a lot of money traveling – running away from relationships back at home into the uncertainty of greener pastures. I wanted to be happy. I wanted to be fulfilled. I couldn't explain what, but I wanted something more.

Stranger number 5 didn't have to explain her loneliness or lack of clarity around happiness and fulfillment. I completely got it. I had been there.

Sitting on the cold stone steps above the downtown beauty of historic Prague, I thought I was doomed to a lifelong journey alone. Somehow I got out of that struggle and into a place of puppy love, marriage, and a young family of my own. Even still, a part of me fears that tomorrow I might wake up in an empty bed and have my life, as it is now, evaporate like an early morning dream – leaving me wondering if it happened at all. Or, that some unforeseen event could strip this away from me and I will be left alone, throwing bread crumbs to the starving birds by myself for the rest of my life.

Stranger number 5 said she's like a wave coming in and going back out.

Waves will throw us with fury onto the land, before sucking us back into the cold depths of uncertain and sometimes violent waters. We can thrash and struggle through the turbulent ride. Or, we can let the current steer us and take solace in the knowledge that another wave will eventually come along and carry us back to shore where there is another chance to grab hold and a chance that the stability and comfort of a soft sandy beach will become our home.

STRANGER 6

"The family is a haven in a heartless world."
- Christopher Lasch

Thousands of miles separated her and her family because she chose to go westward looking for new opportunity. After realizing the opportunity wasn't what she had hoped, she held on until she returned to the comfort of her family.

My stomach had stretched beyond its capacity. The only thing I needed was to undo the top button on my pants and curl up on the couch in the lobby of the luxurious hotel we had just eaten at.

Close friends had invited us to join them for a Valentine's weekend brunch – that inevitably led to another case of over indulgence. My plan for this week's stranger was to find someone sitting in the lobby of the hotel to interview, but my wife and I decided it was probably best if we went for a little stroll to get some fresh air and attempt to work off a few thousand calories.

It was a chilly Sunday afternoon and walking turned naturally into shopping as the store front windows lured us in with their cunning signs that screamed "50% off!" My wife, Erin, dove into the bargain racks. I was still feeling the after effects of the large quantity of brunch, so I wandered back into the fresh air outside.

Outside, I found a young woman standing alone. She appeared as though she was waiting for someone. I watched to see if she was going anywhere, and she remained still and solo. I assumed she was waiting for me, so I meandered over to her, made my pitch, and started a great conversation.

In just under 12 minutes, Stranger 6 had shown me a full gamut of emotions: belly laughing to complete tears. She was bright and cheerful – a 24-year-old retail worker who missed home dearly. She had left the east coast and traveled across the country seeking adventure and wanting to experience life in the West.

1) What is your dream job?

"Veterinarian, right now. Yes. And, I would be willing to pay the $100,000 to go to school for it. I've always liked animals – they've always liked me. Hissing cats, it's like 'OK, whatever' go on about their business. That's what I originally went to school for, but $16,000 a year and student loans wouldn't cover so I couldn't go back for a second year. I've always liked them. They're more honest than most people, so I find that they're easier to work with."

2) What fulfills you?

"Animals. They're always there. I mean, right now I have one guinea pig. My dog is back home. He's 11 years old, no teeth, arthritis, his kidneys are going, and he's going blind. Working with animals would be awesome – that's basically everything. If I could get into that I'd be the happiest person in the world. I could live in the dumps and be happy doing that."

3) What is your greatest fear?

"Losing my family. Losing contact with them. I call my mother everyday. I moved away and she bought a puppy to replace me because we're so close. I think if I ever lost (my family) I would lose my mind. I'd be one of the crazy people you see walking around the street muttering to themselves, twitching, and then lashing out at you when you walk past them."

4) What do you want more of in your life?

"Family. I will actually be back home at the end September – going back to school, hopefully. If not, I'm still going back. The city (Calgary) is nice, but I hate the people. Two strangers on a bus, both of them (from back home), are the only people I've talked to in Calgary – outside of the group of friends who brought me here. So, I'm going back."

5 a) What is your greatest accomplishment?

"I think right now my greatest accomplishment is that I'm here – that I'm staying here until September and not going back before. And, I will stay here until September and I will put up with it. This is something I did on my own, and so I'm really proud of that. I came away from the family. I'll regret the experience for the rest of my life (laughing), but I'm glad I came out here. It's fun – it's not a bad city it's just the people I have an issue with that's all."

5 b) What are you most ashamed of?

"That I didn't enjoy it more – That I didn't put myself out more to hang out with my friends and even look for a different job. Because, this (job) that I transferred in from the other store that I was working at was just retail and, like, I'm really good. Manager sucks, oh my god! But, you know I'm really ashamed at myself that I didn't go and look for a different job and go in a different field and see how I did in that."

6) What makes you sad?

"Not having my family here. If I had them here it would be a lot easier. We're very close. A lot of people who are out here don't understand that. They're like, 'I don't understand how you can call your mother every day.' I can have, like, four hour conversations with my mother and call her four days in a row and have four hour (conversations). We talk about the family and my little brother, my Dad, the pets, my sister. Like, there's lots of things, the rest of the family, how my Nan's doing. Because they're all on the east coast, right? So, and I don't get to see none of them out here either. But, not having my family here."

7) What is the hardest thing you have experienced?

"My Grandfather – he passed away from a heart attack. They wouldn't operate on him, they refused to do it. So when his a ...sorry (weeping). The fourth stroke he died and I wasn't there and I've only ever seen him once. I met him once in my entire life and then he was gone. You regret what you don't have, but I'm glad I met him. I couldn't understand a damn word he said, but I'm glad I met him."

8) What is great about you?

"I'm very blunt and opinionated. My friends call me the 'Krista Buddha' because I'm extremely comfortable with myself. I am, as you can see, overweight and I don't care. I love food to much to put it down to go with someone else's expectations of myself. My friends value that about me, and I value that about myself. I trust myself to be able to tell someone 'your being an idiot and I will smack you for it' and they know they can come to me and I will be truthful with them. Whether it hurts or not, I will tell them the truth and they really do appreciate that. That's what I think is the greatest thing about me."

9) Who are you?

"I'm like the moss growing on the 'lee' side of the tree out of the sun. Almost always when you look there – I'll be there. As a friend you know that's who I am. If you need someone to go to, something to lean on – it's there. It's always soft, it's always there if you look on the dark side of the tree, there's always that little green thing growing on the side because there's not enough sun light. I don't handle the sun very well – I'm actually slightly allergic to it."

I had just over twelve minutes with 'Krista Buddha'. Twelve minutes doesn't seem long a long time, but it was long enough for her to share laughter and shed tears with me, a complete stranger.

'Krista Buddha' is thousands of miles away from her family, but the connection remains strong. I was touched by her desire to maintain a deep loving relationship with her family despite the distance between them.

I've never ventured far away from my family for long amounts of time. For years I traveled at months on end when I was competing internationally in sports, but my home base was never far away from my family. In fact it's quite the opposite. After initially moving away from home in search of freedom, I find myself inching closer to them as time passes. My family are my friends and I have kept them close.

There was a time, less than four years ago, when I was really struggling. My best friend had passed away, I failed to reach the Olympics for the second time, and I just wanted to throw open the windows and scream at the unjust world. My family stood beside me through all of it. The greatest and most tragic moments of my life have been shared with my family. They are not just the people I've grown up with. I feel they have been my teammates through the glorious and most challenging circumstances of my life.

Family is the central tribe that supports us through the greatest and most challenging periods of our lives. This tribe consists of blood family, close friends, and mentors who help shape and support us – those who share laughter and tears and challenge us to grow.

Family is not only a haven in a what sometimes seems like a heartless world, but the oars on each side of the boat – working together to move forward, facing strong winds head on, keeping steady through the storms and sharing in the celebration of new discoveries.

STRANGER 7

"We need you, we need your youth, your strength, and your idealism, to help us make right what is wrong"
- Ronald Reagan

Abandoned by his father when he was eight years old, Stranger 7 grew up struggling internally with his relationship with his father. With only months leading up to his high school graduation, he would have to face him again.

I can be a procrastinator. In the spirit of bettering myself and in an effort to stop driving Erin crazy (with my frantic late Sunday night editing for Monday's blog), I decided to allow myself plenty of time to prepare for this week's entry. I started my search for Stranger number 7 on Thursday afternoon.

Even though the downtown lunch rush had passed, there were still people lingering around the food court area in a downtown market. A debonair looking business man in his early forties was sitting by himself reading the daily tidbits from a newspaper. I nervously shuffled over to him, gave him my pitch, and quickly found out he wasn't the least bit interested. I refused to let this derail me, so I forged ahead – ego slightly bruised, but battle tested and ready for the next one.

I spotted a sweet looking old man, who appeared to be in his eighties, sitting solo on a wooden bench outside the food court. Feeling confident, I shimmied up beside him and kindly delivered my proposal into his discreet hearing aid. Never in my life has anyone looked at me with such utter disgust. I quickly darted away fearing he would unsheathe his cane.

Friday and Saturday passed quickly with no success and my attempts to enroll Stranger 7, up to this point, had dismally failed. Erin was going to have to put up with the clickety-clacking of my Mac book keys until the early hours of Monday morning.

I left the house mid-day on Sunday to run errands – my first stop was to return videos. After returning a disappointing selection from last week, I went in search of a classic 80s flick. Having no luck finding what I was looking for, I went to the front desk to ask for some help. The young man working the computer greeted me warmly as I approached the counter. He had long dark hair pulled into a pony tail that stretched down his back. His hairstyle, coupled with a dark goatee, made him appear much older than he actually was – as I soon found out.

I asked him about *The Breakfast Club*. They only had copies for sale, not to rent. So, I asked for his expert advice. Immediately he walked from behind the counter and started speaking enthusiastically about a few older DeNiro movies from the late seventies. It just so happened that I hadn't seen either of them. So, I took his advice and grabbed them from the shelf.

There we stood, amidst racks of movies without another customer in sight. I reached into my pocket and grabbed my digital voice recorder – I wasn't about to let this stranger get away. Before he turned to walk back behind the counter, I asked him if he'd be interested in my experiment. Within seconds, I was deep in a meaningful conversation with a seventeen-year-old high school senior.

1) What is your dream job?

"Probably an archeologist in Iceland – study some of the old Viking relics. It's where my family comes from and Iceland is one of the most beautiful countries on this planet. And, everything like that – to just see all that. I've been a fan of archeology and interested in it since I was five years old and I remember going out and doing a dig when I was a kid. It was just amazing. So, doing something like that – checking out my family history in Iceland would be amazing. Doing something like that and getting paid for it would be incredible."

2) What fulfills you?

"Whenever I accomplish something that I set my mind towards. Like, when I actually do something that I set my mind towards and then I actually finish it. That's a pretty fulfilling thing."

3) What is your greatest fear?

"I have a fear of heights and I have a fear of deep water – which is weird. I don't know where that got started. Probably complete isolation. That's a really big one. I've never been really truly alone in my entire life, so that complete isolation would be terrifying."

4) What do you want more of in your life?

"More money – that's one. I have dreams. I gotta go to university. I gotta… and I only work a part time job. I work two shifts a week. That's just a physical one, but if I really boiled it down I'd want more interpersonal relationships – more friends, something like that."

5 a) What is your greatest accomplishment?

"I haven't accomplished all that much. Probably being accepted into the U of C. That's an academic accomplishment in today's day and age. U of C is over packed, so you gotta get in there – It's pretty tough. So, I think that's a pretty big one for me."

5 b) What are you most ashamed of?

"Probably that I didn't get to know my great grandfather well enough before he passed away. Because, I mean, I was a kid and I didn't really realize the significance of what he was saying until after he was gone. So, that's a pretty big one actually."

6) What makes you sad?

"The world – everything about it. The pitiful state of affairs that we live in nowadays – it's depressing. I mean, you look around there's crime, there's violence, everything that's going on – it's going down the hole. The neighborhood I live in used to be amazing and now it's just kinda degrading. Our society is degrading at an ever growing rate and it's really depressing actually. Just the state of the youth in our nation and everything, it just depresses me more than anything. Looking at people my age, it's ridiculous. It's not even worth it some days to think about."

7) What is the hardest thing you have ever experienced?

"Probably, coming to terms with my relationship with my father. That's a pretty big one. Because, he left me and my mom when I was, like, 8 years old and he wasn't that good to me. So, just coming to terms with that. And, now he's coming to my graduation in May and all that. So, that's been pretty tough."

8) What is great about you?

"Normally I could go on an egotistical tangent, but my immediate thought was my hair – just for fun. I don't know. My ability to really make relationships, to make really strong bonds with people, my musical ability – I would say that would be a really great thing about me. I don't know. There is a lot of things, but I don't want to be, like, too egotistical. I'm intelligent. I'm funny – like, I've made you laugh a couple times already. So, there's plenty of stuff, but that could apply to anybody."

9) Who are you?

"Just another person. I would just describe me as just another person because there is nothing really significant about anybody, if you were really to boil it down. So, if you want to remember me you have to make your own impression instead of me trying to make one for you."

10) What question do you want me to ask you now?

"What kind of life I've led"

What kind of life have you led?

"Now I have to think about it. I didn't really think of the answer before I thought of the question. I've led, generally, a good life – I believe. But, everybody has their own rules and all that and I feel that I've tried to balance out the two in my life. And yet in the end, I don't think I ever actually will balance out the two perfectly – which, is a little disconcerting as a human."

While looking for Stranger 7, I couldn't believe that I had nothing to show but a pocketful of rejections when Sunday morning arrived. In hindsight, it worked out for the best because I ended up with the perfect Stranger. His answers were articulate. His thoughts were insightful. However, I disagree with his outlook on the world.

I agree it can be cruel. The violence in the world seems to be never ending – as constant as the rising and setting of the sun. Many people can be disrespectful and display entitlement. Materialism has besieged everyday life and people race faster and faster to acquire 'things' they expect will make their lives happier. The culmination of all of this can dampen even the brightest spirits. But, I still have hope. I have hope for the future because of individuals like Stranger 7.

He says he couldn't, or wouldn't answer question 9: Who are you? So, I'll take his advice and make my own impression.

Stranger 7 is intelligent, creative, humble, and funny. My guess is that he has been raised very well. He treats others with respect and dignity and he ponders the larger issues in life. There is a strong compassionate side to him and he exudes a courageous confidence that really drew me in. He is strong and independent. He's a musician that lives life walking to the beat of his own drum. He is more than "just another person." Stranger 7 is a young Viking. Like Leif Erikson, he battles the cold temperatures of the planet and braves the uncertainty of the future – seeking the warmth and refuge of a new world. Stranger 7 is young, strong, and idealistic. He is the future that can help us make right what is wrong.

STRANGER 8

"Kites rise highest against the wind, not with it."
- Winston Churchill

The rusty yellow light bulb hung from a thin string and swung slowly from side to side making barely enough light to see. The thick stone walls held beads of cold sweat and the pungent smell of mold ran up my nostrils with each nervous breath. My wrists were bound with wire to the thick oak chair I was placed in. Standing on the other side of the table, a man peered at me in disgust. He took a drag from his cigarette then sent it flying into the corner – creating a blast of sparks amongst the darkness. His steps made a slight echo in the cold stone room as he moved closer to me. I could smell the fresh smoke on his breath as he leaned over top of me. With a raspy mid-western voice, he said, "You've got to ask yourself one question: Do I feel lucky? Well, do ya punk?"
Stop the interrogation! I'm the one who is doing the interview!

I had a just finished a meeting at popular shopping centre, so I went for a stroll through the mall in search of Stranger 8. Immediately, I targeted a sophisticated looking middle-aged man sitting alone on a bench scrolling through his blackberry. He wore a long black coat and a crimson scarf hung loosely around his neck.

I became nervous. I don't know what it is about middle-aged professionals but, at times, I find it intimidating to approach them. However, if something intimidates me I take it on as a challenge. So, I walked up to this executive looking man and made my pitch.

This was my most challenging experience yet.

He slowly lifted his eyes off his blackberry and peered up at me like a disapproving parent. With a quiet but vicious tone (a bit like Clint Eastwood), he skeptically fired questions my way:

"What is this social experiment?"

"What will you do with this?"

"Why are you doing this?"

"Are you even educated to be a life coach?"

"What kind of education do you need to be a life coach?"

"Do you have a degree?"

"What is this for?"

"How does someone become a life coach?"

"How long will this take?"

My heart raced inside my chest. In fact, it was beating so hard it wanted to burst out of my chest and run for cover – inside a shoe box at the footwear store behind me. My vocation was being attacked. I was being attacked. My credibility and integrity were all being attacked.

Despite my feelings inside, I remained calm, focused on my breath, and tried to answer his questions to the best of my ability. I explained how successful the experiment had been working so far, and that if he was willing he would be Stranger 8. He softened his stance somewhat and agreed to participate.

Victory was mine. I was emotionally spent, exhausted, scuffed up, and ready to hit the showers. Only, the game was just beginning with this gentleman – a fifty year old oil business owner who we'll call Mr. E.

1) What is your dream job?

"Probably what I'm doing right now with a little bit more building development. I guess, architecture in general. I've built some projects and I enjoy doing that. So, that's what I really enjoy, but I enjoy what I'm doing now too."

2) What fulfills you?

"Health, sports, and family. Once you've got health you've got everything else. Without that you're kind of behind the eight ball. You've got to have a good family. You've got to have a good connection with people. I do lots of sports."

Why are sports fulfilling for you?

"It's because you're never done I guess. At the end of the day you're always trying to be better, or faster, stronger. It's fun."

3) What is your greatest fear?

"Greatest fear? I have to think about that one. I'm not really sure I've got one. Gosh, I've never given that any thought, fear."

Nothing jumps out?

"Not at all."

4) What do you want more of in your life?

"Maybe a little more time. Probably, travel a little bit more. I'd do that. But, other than that I think I'm pretty balanced right now."

5 a) What is your greatest accomplishment?

"Greatest accomplishment would be probably running the business that I'm in right now. I started it, built it, and continue to run the company I'm in now. So, probably one of my greatest."

5 b) What are you most ashamed of?

"Probably, not striving for a high enough education."

6) What makes you sad?

"Elderly care – it just makes me sad to be honest. I've got a parent that's older and I think they could have better care. And, I see a lot of other people who have parents that could have better care and it makes me sad."

7) What's the hardest thing you have ever experienced?

"Probably a divorce, (dealing with) lawyers."

8) What's great about you?

"I'm a pretty balanced guy. My lifestyle I guess. I've had a great life so far – traveled the world, done a lot of stuff, lots of balance."

9) Who are you?

"I am 'Mr. E.' and proud to say that I am that person and will remain that person for the rest of my life. That's who I am. I'm a father, I'm a son, I'm an uncle, all of those things."

10) What question do you want me to ask you now?

"I'm not sure what the bottom line is to the questions. I mean, you can ask somebody a question, but be prepared for the answer. And, you have to have something – with that answer you have to be prepared to do something with it, in my mind, or else the process is kind of moot, in my mind. I think I could ask the people in my circles those questions. Again, I'm just not sure where that would be going."

Mr. E was undeniably my most difficult encounter yet. I had to really dig to get him to open up to me. I could see a struggle happening behind his eyes with each new question. My guess is that the struggle wasn't due to the difficulty of the questions – it was due to the uncomfortable place the questions took him.

Despite the intimidating introduction and beginning to our meeting, I am grateful I had the opportunity to interview Mr. E because he forced me to explain myself in ways I hadn't experienced in previous interviews. The barrage of questions caught me off guard, but left me better prepared for the next round. Not only that – they have strengthened my confidence and reaffirmed the impact and education this experiment has for myself and others.

52 people is about challenges and opposition. It is about discomfort. I've spent most of my life going with the wind in my relationships and avoiding conversations which I feared would be uncomfortable. With a challenge comes learning, and with learning comes growth. If we never face the wind we will never learn, and if we never learn we can never grow.

Stranger 8 challenged me on the purpose and motive of my questions. He saw no meaning to them. The questions are just questions and the answers are just answers. What is important is the space between the question and answer – that creates the purpose and connection between two people. This is the place where opportunity meets the fear of transparency. The place we simultaneously desire and fear. The place that forces you to turn and face the wind. The place where you are challenged with something new.

When faced with life's challenges, some will turn away and hide from the wind in an effort to protect their kite from damage. Others will squint face first into the ferocity of the gale and toss the fragile kite into the freedom of the sky. If you have the courage to confront the wind, you eventually become skilled at guiding the spindle despite the unpredictable wind – controlling the fervor in which the kite climbs higher, cutting and thrashing through the tides of air. You champion your growth by choosing to step into the wind and by letting the kite fly as high as your courage will allow.

STRANGER 9

"The best and most beautiful things in the world cannot be seen or touched. They must be felt with the heart."
- Helen Keller

A family huddled close together underground in complete darkness. Their hungry bellies, parched lips, and eyes yearned to feel the warmth of sunlight. They were not hiding from the anger of Mother Nature and her power to inflict earthquakes or tsunamis. They hid from bombs and bullets.

It was just after 5 a.m. and I peeked out the front window of my house to see the taxi roll up. My wife and I were extremely under dressed since we anticipated the Floridian weather, not the cold snowy morning that had unexpectedly greeted us. Battling the frigid temperatures, we quickly loaded our luggage and jumped into the cab.

Our taxi driver was about mid-thirties with dark hair and large kind eyes. He thought he was only picking up clients to run them to the airport. However, the crisp winter air on this morning brought him more than destination sun seekers. The taxi cab driver had no idea he'd be Stranger number 9.

1) What is your dream job?

"Stay home, sit on the couch – (laugh) that would be the best thing to do. Being able to take care of my kids, maybe stay home with them, drive them where ever they want to go – that's of course if all the resources are there. Anybody could have whatever he wants. Doesn't have to work – I guess would be an ideal thing right?"

2) What fulfills you?

"When you have a good health, good family, good surroundings, no stress, that's basically it. What's question number three?"

3) What is your greatest fear?

"Maybe to lose a kid, or something happen to my kids."

4) What do you want more of in your life?

"Generally, I'm satisfied with what I have. Being work and everything, but of course I wish the best or better for my kids, to be better, or to live a better life. More money. A little bit more money doesn't hurt. I would use it for the necessity things: education, this stuff."

5 a) What is your greatest accomplishment?

"I don't know what to tell you. The greatest thing basically that happened to me: coming to Canada. After living most of my life in Lebanon under the ground in shelters during the war, that could be the greatest thing actually."

5 b) What are you most ashamed of?

"Since I've been seventeen years old I never done something I'm ashamed of. Maybe before that I didn't listen a bit for my parents, but other than that…"

6) What makes you sad?

"To see people around me sometimes sad, or when I see people die and nobody cares –nobody gives a damn about it."

7) What is the hardest thing you have ever experienced?

"The loss of my brothers life, basically. My younger brother died at an early age. He didn't have anything to do with anything and just being in the wrong time. The wrong place at the wrong time – that's it."

8)What is great about you?

"That I'm calm. I'm a calm person. I don't get angry very easy. That's a good thing I guess."

9) Who are you?

"A satisfied person. A satisfied person – I have no complaints in life."

10) What question do you want me to ask you now?

"To be honest, I don't know. You ask the questions. (*nothing pops into your head?*) Nothing pops into my head."

Will you ask these questions to the people closest to you in your life?

"I might ask some few questions. But, my personality – I don't ask too many questions. If I want to say something I relate to life experience or something that happened or something that been done maybe on a positive note or a negative note. So, I relate my advice or my disappointment – I don't base it on a theory question. I like to base everything on a fact – on something that happened, and it's been proven, and it has a positive or negative impact. So that's what I like to get – especially with my kids. I have a fourteen-year-old son. When I talk to him, I like to base everything on something he can see. Not on a theory that could happen, could not happen. Not when you give some most of the time examples of something that happened or been done. It makes a lot more sense."

Stranger 9 left his country of Lebanon in 1991, just after the civil war had ended. With most of his family, he arrived in Montreal where he spent two years before finally landing in Calgary in the late part of 1993. He was a licensed taxi driver for fourteen years, but a dream to own his own business put the brakes on the cab industry. He sold his condo and sunk his life savings into a small snack shop which operated successfully in the down town core for several years. The lease for his business expired during the peak of the economic boom and the outrageous new rates left him unable to afford the space. He lost his business, the boom took a downward direction, and the space has remained empty ever since.

Stranger 9 spoke about educating his son and the importance of providing him with a certain type of education – an education based on facts, something proven, or something tangible that you can see. Are we a society fascinated by IQ (intelligence quotient) at the expense of EQ (emotional quotient)? How do we strike a balance?

During our interview I was really drawn to his big green eyes. His eyes had an energetic wisdom about them. An energy that told a story with a calm strength developed through his experiences in life: Undocumented theories tested and proven and trial and error with both failure and success. Theories, tests – all of these moments fill a kaleidoscope full of emotions that shaped those experiences for him. When we think of memories from our past, the ones that stick out are those that conjure up the most emotion. No matter how hard we try, we can't physically touch these memories or lessons. We spend much of our lives cramming to remember things for exams that we eventually forget. We always remember the experiences that create the greatest emotion.

The pain, love, anger, sadness, joy, fear: all these emotions shape the true meaning of the greatest lessons I've learned in my life. Our greatest lessons, experiences, and dreams are not something that can be understood by fact, by touching, or by seeing. Deep learning and true meaning are developed through the deep experience of emotion.

They cannot be graded. They must be felt in the heart.

STRANGER 10

"Faith makes all things possible... love makes all things easy."
- Dwight L. Moody

A scar on his chest exposed the evidence of heart surgery six years prior. Eighty-four years old and shirtless in the hot sun, he proudly wore white shorts and a Team Canada Hockey hat. Pointing to his hat he said, "I was born in Italy, but Canada is my country."

I closed my eyes and felt the intense heat pour over my body. The hot Florida sun beat down on us as we sprawled out like a giant pod of sea lions on the pool deck. Golden brown bodies surrounded me and the sounds of children playing and splashing in the pool filled my ears. I basked in the sun and read my book while an older man slowly shuffled up and chose the pool chair just inches away from mine. We began a light conversation while he spent close to five minutes engaged in the process of sitting down. Once he was in place he turned to me, reached over, and tickled my feet. I had made a new friend.

Now that we had developed a bond, I asked him to be Stranger 10. He stared intently at me. "I'll tell you anything," he said with strength and conviction. "I've got nothing to hide."

Just then, Cicero's wife of 57 years walked up to speak to him. Before she had a chance to speak, he interrupted to tell her about our interview. She looked over at me apologetically, smiled, and patted me on the knee. "He has a lot of answers."

1) What is your dream job?

"To be healthy, strong, mind my own business, and love people. Health is the main thing isn't it? Without health you're sick – you're done. Now second question."

2) What fulfills you?

"I get up first thing in the morning and I say to God, 'You are the Creator. You are the best and I beg you and pray you to keep me strong and healthy.'"

49

3) What is your greatest fear?

"Well, I'm not afraid to die, but I don't like to die now really, if I can help it. Only God knows when my time is up. If my time is up my time is up – nothing you can do about it, right? That's how I feel. What do you think? I don't disturb anybody, I don't bother anybody, and I don't do bad things against anybody. So, my conscience is free and clear. I don't have to worry about it."

4) What do you want more of in your life?

"To be kind with my family, enjoy my family, and love them and know it is a great gift. My family – I have a son and three daughters, ten grandchildren at home in Windsor – I love them and want to see them grow."

5 a) What is your greatest accomplishment?

"To meet my wife, love her, and bring a family into this world. We have been married for 57 years. It is not easy these days, believe you me. You see nothing but separations, divorce, and live together. No, we did it together, but we were married in a Italian church, a Catholic church in Windsor."

5 b) What are you most ashamed of?

"The way humans are today: killing, murdering, don't get along, fight, war. For me: not a thing. I'm proud of my life. I never hurt anybody and I didn't mind anyone's business but my own – this is why I'm so happy because I have nothing to fear, nothing."

6) What makes you sad?

"Well, when something's wrong in the family you can't be happy. You are not going to say – joy! So, it would make me very upset. Sometimes I even dream at night something is wrong. I yell at night. I'm very sensitive in that department. That's how I feel."

7) What is the hardest thing you have ever experienced?

"That's a tough question. When I started working in the tool and dye shop in '56. The employer hired me and he said, 'I give you a chance – dollar an hour to start and if you improve, more money.' I was afraid not to make it and I did. I used my strong will and my strong feeling to do the best as I can. Everything I had in my body I put into to make myself something special and provide for my family. It was my responsibility to take care of my family."

8) What is great about you?

"Well I'm not going to tap my own shoulder. Well, I'm pretty proud of one thing: I was a good father with the right help and I love my family. Not only for me, but my neighbours and friends. I was not jealous of anything. And, the way I feel – I'm pretty proud of that."

9) Who are you?

"I'm a human being – from my mother and my father, which I love them so much. But nothing special to me, just a human being. It's all I can tell you. Special to me is nothing. I love to take care of my family. I love being nice with people. I love to be kind and I don't tend to offend anybody."

10) What question do you want me to ask you now?

"Do I believe in God?"

Do you believe in God?

"I do – I do believe in God. He is the creator. Who created the universe? God – not Galileo Galilei, the astronomer. It has to be something. Who makes everything possible? Who creates, as I said, the globe, the mountains, the sea, living, us? There has to be something on the other side of the world. We never see them, but if we do have faith, we believe, and we said he's the one. I don't know if you are Catholic or not – that's your business. I am Catholic and I take care of my religion. I profess my religion is the right one. I'm not fanatic – those people just show off. But, I was raised Catholic. My parents taught me this way and I feel this way. I'm not here to tell you Catholic religion is the best – we have our problems too."

Cicero was born in 1927 in Northern Italy, 15 miles from Cortina D'empezzo – a place I visited frequently while racing on the World Cup bobsleigh tour. The eleventh of twelve children, he grew up on a farm working with his siblings in the fields where everyone contributed to the family's well-being. He was one of two boys. He worked hard in the fields until he was drafted into the Italian army when he was 19. After spending 18 months in the army, he joined his family as they packed up for a different life in Canada. It was in Canada that Cicero met his future wife, built a family, and spent the next 35 years working at a tool and dye shop.

I spotted Cicero lounging by the pool each day during the rest of our stay. Sometimes we'd engage in brief conversations. Other times we'd just give each other a collegial nod as if we were brothers from an exclusive society sharing esoteric secrets.

Cicero spoke of faith and love often.

I could sense the love he has for his wife, children, grandchildren, and others who are close to him. He told me of the struggles he and his wife went through, and the peaks and valleys of marital life. He said love alone helped them through the tough times. He spoke early and often about his pledge and devotion to Catholicism. His faith provided him with the support needed to cross the Atlantic Ocean with his family and start from scratch in a land of strangers.

What I admired about his religious devotion was that he was open minded enough to accept me regardless of my spiritual affiliation. He didn't ask, he didn't try to sell me on it, and it didn't matter. He possesses the wisdom to understand that by choosing his faith his choice alone is all that matters. His choice and devotion is his faith. His faith is not obstructed nor enhanced by the approval or rejection from a complete stranger.

Each morning during his vacation, Cicero sat shirtless, facing squint-eyed into the sun. One early afternoon, I noticed the bright red skin on his chest, so I alerted him.

"Cicero, it might be time for you to put on some sunscreen."

"I love the sun," he blurted emotionless, without opening his eyes to see who was speaking to him. I guess, after 84 years on this planet – trusting his faith to make things possible, he has the wisdom to rely on his love to sooth the pain of even the deepest sun burn.

STRANGER 11

"All men's miseries derive from not being able to sit in a quiet room alone."
- Blaise Pascal

She used to run from it until she did the most difficult thing – stood face to face with it, embraced it, and sat with it.

We were at a viewing of the documentary 'The Science of Miracles' based on a book by computer scientist and author Gregg Braden. Braden discussed the quantum language of healing, peace, feeling, and belief. For the parts I was awake for, it seemed quite compelling. I had trouble keeping my eyes open throughout the movie. My wife would periodically squeeze my fingers when I started to snore lightly – making me snap my head up and focus for a brief moment before spacing out again. It was an interesting documentary, but I was exhausted and the soothing voice of Gregg Braden had cast a spell on my eyelids. I did my best to call upon on the facial Three Musketeers: Levator, Frontalis, and Meuller, to join together and combat the sorcerer of sleep. It was a battle that would have continued for some time if peace had not arrived through the salvation of the light switch.

We stuck around for a while after the show and perused the book section at the back of the church, where the film showing had taken place. Hundreds of books, DVDs and CDs relating to self-help, healing modalities and spirituality were available for purchase.

Behind one of the tables, there was a volunteer who appeared to be about fifty-years-old. Her silver and white hair hung just above her shoulders and her vibrant greyish-blue eyes shone behind a thin pair of glasses. I snuck up beside a friend of mine who was engaged in a conversation with her – curious about what they were speaking of. Our eyes met and instantly I knew she would be Stranger number 11. We spoke for a short while before I asked if I could interview her. Moments later, I was leaning against the bookshelf engaged in a conversation with the woman behind the counter – Brida.

1) What is your dream job?

"More of what I'm doing in a bigger way. I'm involved in humanitarian business and I'm involved in spiritual and personal empowerment – taking that bigger, deeper, wider. That would look like me having my writing published and my songs published and having that website that, you know, I still haven't developed – actually develop it. Find a way to allow total 'me' into total 'we'."

2) What fulfills you?

"Doing what I'm doing: being present to allowing my own personal time and attention to my own personal journey. Very much me, and then taking that out there and allowing me to be a part of the bigger picture and how it interweaves with the we that I'm involved in."

3) What is your greatest fear?

"That I won't get at all that stuff that I... that I'll leave some of my music inside of me. Wayne Dyer, in one of the movies that was played here (at the church), he made a decision for himself: 'Wayne, don't die with your music still inside of you.'"

4) What do you want more of in your life?

"More of what I've got. Learning how to love what is – practicing that process. Understanding that if everything is happening for a purpose that I may not understand and can I love what is right here and right now and consciously be with the gifts that are being offered and notice the subconscious awareness that is being revealed by what's happening in my world. So stepping more into that – being with what loving is."

5a) What is your greatest accomplishment?

"Besides having two amazing children who are 25 and 23 who everyone tells me are amazing – those aren't my words those are other people's words. Besides those two children, my main accomplishment is stepping forward out of non-conscious living onto a pathway of practicing that – more conscious living."

5b) What are you most ashamed of?

"A few years ago, I had an experience of being able to be loved in a group setting in a spiritual weekend. Some of them from San Diego came up and I asked if the group would love me as 'shame'. So, I had a part of me that felt shame – a young part about five years old that felt shame and she had developed this identity of herself in shame, so she didn't know anything else. That group sang a song called 'how can anyone ever tell you you're anything less than beautiful, how can anyone ever tell you're anything less than whole.' So, they were singing this song and standing and holding me in love. As I'm standing in front of them crying and being held by a woman who came up and said, 'can I hold you?' Because that was part of her work – was to hold me. Someone came up energetically and kind of held us and I got to be seen and loved in that moment as shame. Without anyone saying, 'oh you shouldn't think that, oh you shouldn't feel that, oh let me fix you,' they just let me be seen in shame and loved as that – as though I didn't know anything else. Do you know since that time I don't have any 'thing' that I'm most ashamed of because now I can just go, 'well there is shame somewhere in everyone's life I believe. Can I allow that, whatever it is, and still love myself? Know I'm worthy.' And…yeah so, that was a very powerful life shifting moment for me."

6) What makes you sad?

"Well, a couple of things that have made me sad in the last few years is the sense of overwhelm for needs of the world. Look at the world and the statistics and know that in a 24-hour period 30,000 children under the age of five have died from water-borne diseases, starvation, and AIDS. I had a great sense of overwhelm in that need and in my work. I was a physical therapist and have moved more into the mind, body, spirit work. People I was seeing were feeling overwhelmed and in such need. I would get kind of sad, well quite sad, in that sense of overwhelm and 'how the heck am I going to make a difference in the world?' So, that would tend to make me very sad."

7) What is the hardest thing you have ever experienced?

"The hardest thing I have experienced to this point in this lifetime was a sexualized abuse relationship with a grandfather when I was 4 1/2 years old, and then all of the beliefs that I created about myself and the world as a result of that relationship. So, that's the hardest untruth. Bruce Lipton has a book here, The Biology of Belief, and he was talking about, how up to about the age of six we are in what is called a hypnologic state and what goes in as a child we usually take on just as if it's a part of who we are now. Unless we find a way to say, 'oh that's not true.' A lot of us have tied into the sense of separation of 'I'm alone' and victimhood. And so, (overcoming) those hypnologic suggestions that were created by my belief as a young child, but then carried into adolescence and adulthood, that's been my greatest challenge."

8) What is great about you?

"I'm willing to, now in my life, be spirit – showing up as act of love. I was in meditation a few years ago and I (asked), 'spirit what is mine to do?' And the answer was 'be my love in action Brida, be my love in action.'

'Oh!' I said, 'give me something. Give me a book to write or something, but you know 'be my love in action?' What am I supposed to do with that?'

'No, Brida there is nothing else. Just, would you be my love in action, in this breath? Would you be my love in action right now?' It just kept repeating that and repeating that.

The greatest thing about me, I would say, is that I'm practicing that at a much more conscious level."

9) Who are you?

"I am god expressing through a human body, and a human personality with all of the experiences that I've collected along the way that give me this. Like these – I wear glasses – so my personality has a visual field that encompasses every belief that I have about myself that is expressing. But, I believe the truth of who I am is divine expression on planet earth at this moment in time."

10) What question do you want me to ask you now?

"I'm just getting what's in your heart – that's the question that spirit has for me, whatever is in your heart. I'm not hearing a question; I'm hearing a sound, like the heart chakra sound. That sound is like the base note of the universe."

There was a point in time in my life when I was running – running from pain, running from fear, running from the reality of life. I hid it fairly well – at least I think I hid it well – but the suffering inside me burned deep. I wasn't sure how to deal with it, but I did know one thing – I couldn't be with it. I found several ways to escape the pain. Hard training, frequent traveling, late-night parties, and video games all distracted me from the reality of grief and suffering – from the reality of my situation and where I was in life. The irony is the harder I tried to run away the stronger my suffering became. The walls I put up became thicker and higher – leaving me a prisoner in my own cell, a cell I had found myself trapped in, not realizing that I also held the only key out.

When we fully allow ourselves to experience emotion, we see things in a different way. Our deep-rooted feelings, if unacknowledged, will follow us: our fears and pain will continue to chase us if we run from it. What we resist persists. Or even worse, we push the emotion so deep inside, unwilling to acknowledge its presence until it rears its ugly head – manifesting as a disease. As the saying goes, the body will shed the tears the eyes refuse to weep.

When we sit in a quiet room and allow ourselves to be overcome with our emotion, only then can we truly overcome our pain and leave it behind us. We throw our microscope over top of it and find out it isn't the big bad thing we thought it was.

Brida had a special moment when she was able to be seen and fully experience her childhood shame. Sitting with this wound allowed her to set herself free. Where do you need to be set free?

We all carry old miseries we have been eluding. Sit with your anger, resentment, fear, or sorrow. Break the cycle of escapism, remove the fear attached to emotions, take the mystery out of misery, and set yourself and your relationships free.

STRANGER 12

"Who speaks of liberty while the human mind is in chains?"
- Francis Wright

A young man in his early thirties, desperately desired to create a family of his own. A physical expressionist, he spread attitude into the lives of others while following his ultimate goal of greatness.

"It's not called break dancing; it's called break," my instructor corrected me.

Six weeks into break lessons and I still didn't know the proper name. But, I do now and I also know that people who break aren't break dancers – they are B-boys, or B-girls.

I'm on a quest not only for meaningful relationships, but always on a quest to improve and expand my abilities – especially in the 'coolness' department. You see, I have always been a short, stocky, muscle bound guy. Hours upon hours in the weight room have contributed to stiff rigid movements, limited flexibility, and extended suffering of the condition of ILS (Invisible Lat Syndrome – walking with my arms out wide to make me look bigger).

While I spent 16 hard years laboring in the weight room to be bigger, stronger, and faster, I always had a secret affinity for the skateboarding, snowboarding, and break (dance) culture. I thought they looked cool. So there I was learning how to be cool and how to break dance, I mean learn to break, at 32 years old.

A friend of mine recruited me to join him and try a break lesson. After the first class, I was sold. My instructor dazzled us with his moves, rhythm, and attitude. He slid and shuffled, spun and stalled – often leaving me with my mouth open and dreaming of the day I could leave people spellbound with an amazing power move (head spin) or impossible stall (one armed hand stand). I was infatuated with my instructor's coolness factor. He gave off the impression that there wasn't a moment in his day where he wasn't cool. I had come to the right spot. I needed to know more.

Stranger 12 is my B-boy coach, break instructor, and the man responsible for undertaking the task of helping me transform into coolness.

1) What is your dream job?

"Music production – creating music for amazing artists, individuals, and just good music to produce. There (are) a few things. I like the arts in general – so creating. I like creating. I like dance, music, paintings, whatever. Music – I just remember ever since I was a kid I just liked music. I just loved music, you know. That's why I'm dancing right now –because of that. And, at the same time I feel I have a knack for creating music – creating original music. That's about it. I see myself as a music producer – mix and mastering music, producing it, and recording other people who have created their own music. Just being behind the board, that's it."

2) What fulfills you?

"First and foremost my health. My passions in life fulfill me: dance and music. After that I would say my wife and my family, my friends. Again that goes in cycle. So again, creating music. Making money from what I love – that also fulfills me. So, doing what I love as my job."

3) What is your greatest fear?

"Okay, this is probably my greatest fear and at the same time it's my poison and my medicine – It's fully my medicine and it's good for me – is criticism. So, I'm afraid of being criticized. But at the same time I know that's the only way I'll improve, so I want it. I want it, but I want... I guess my fear is biased criticism – when someone is trying to criticize me out of spite, as opposed to when someone is actually trying to help me. I love that. But at the same time, I can't stand spiteful criticism and sometimes I'm mixed between the two because I'm thinking maybe that person is doing it out of spite. but that person is probably doing that to help me."

4) What do you want more of in your life?

"Right now, I guess, asking for a kid. So, family. More of my offspring and money. Freedom! Not, not, not money, no sorry, not money

– it's freedom, freedom. I would, if I had more money, I would definitely invest in a nice recording studio and open up my time to produce music. So, I don't want money for the sake of having money. I would travel a lot. Every three months I'd take a week off and travel somewhere with my wife. But, first and foremost, what I want more of in my life is healthy family. More healthy family in my life."

5a) What is your greatest accomplishment?

"Actually I never…I have had many, but my greatest accomplishment would be my health. I guess that's an accomplishment – maintaining my health. But then again, also my marriage, I think, is a great accomplishment for me. Just being in tune – like cooperation, mutual respect. So, love of course is the first spark, but love won't last if there isn't mutual respect. So, having a respectful relationship."

5b) What are you most ashamed of?

(Laughing.) "I guess one of the memories that I, like, I'll never forget is having wet my bed at around when I was ten or eleven years old and strangers found out about it because my older sibling just thought it was funny to share with everybody. So, that was probably my most shameful moment at that time. Right now, if that happened I probably wouldn't care much. Maybe I would. I don't know."

6) What makes you sad?

"What makes me sad is my loved ones lack of ability to get to what they want. For example, if say my parents, they don't have a grand kid yet, and if they, god forbid, one of them passes away without having a grand kid that would make me very sad. That would make me very sad. Same with one of my boys, like you know, great guy, great soul having some kind of a short coming in their life – stuff like that."

7) What is the hardest thing you have ever experienced?

"Seeing my mom cry was the toughest thing. And not at the time, because I was the cause of it. But now that I think of it, I'm like 'that is so sad.' I can just totally picture the whole circumstance. And this was when I was sixteen years old, so I can totally remember it. That must have been…and seeing my brother cry too. My brother (was) crying because I was the cause of that too. Maybe I wasn't the cause, but I feel like I was the cause. Again, I wasn't sad at the time when that happened – my brother crying. I was probably even happy about it, you know, because we were fighting and I said some hurtful things and same with my mom. It was just the circumstances. And then looking back, what makes it hard is knowing how cruel I can be, you know, and trying to hurt somebody out of intention, especially my brother. Because my mom, it wasn't like it was a really bad situation at the time. Just hurting other people, that's it. Hurting other people out of irrational emotion, you know. Not really calming myself down. But like ahhh! I wanna get this person as hard as I can and then two hours later I'm like, oh my god I just did that? That was like somebody else."

8) What is great about you?

"My determination. My stubbornness. Not stubb… my determination and my work ethic. I like to think that I'm a conscious person, I'm aware of, say I'll do something wrong, I'll do it knowing that it's wrong. You know what I mean? Like, littering for example – I know littering is wrong no matter what it is and where it is, but I'll do it and I know this is wrong but I'm just going to do it anyway."

9) Who are you?

"It might sound a little conceited. This is my goal – Greatness."

B-boy spoke about wanting more money, but quickly realized what he truly wanted was freedom. We believe we need money to be free, we need more time in order to do the things we want, and we need to succeed in order to deserve the love of others.

No amount of money, time, love, fast cars, or new vistas can set you free. Nothing external can give you freedom. It must come from within. The secret to open up the iron gates or to remove the handcuffs comes from one action – the realization that you hold the key to your freedom. In the most excruciating circumstances humanity has prevailed by knowing that one's true value cannot be taken hostage. Viktor Frankl, who sat imprisoned in a concentration camp for years during the Second World War, made the choice to be free while inside the camp. He found that all his possessions, his family, and his career could be taken away from him, but he always retained the freedom to choose his attitudes and beliefs. Anything can be taken away from us, but the freedom of creation, expression, and love are born and rise from within.

Very early in class, B-boy told us that break is 90 per cent attitude and 10 per cent dance. The same can be said for life. We can live cookie cutter lives doing what 'should' be done – buying a house, having a family, building equity, saving for retirement. We go through the motions of life until we finally arrive on our deathbeds. It is here we sit, reflecting on our dance while the lonely sound of the violin slowly disappears with the last breath we take.

The music of our lives only plays until the last beat of our heart. How do you want to dance? Do you choose to be a wallflower and resentfully watch others engage in the sweetness of life? Do you rigidly side-step, fearful of what others might think? Or do you lose your inhibitions and let the ecstasy of life fill your veins and allow yourself to dance unencumbered?

STRANGER 13

"Every Intention sets energy into motion whether you are conscious of it or not."
- Gary Zukav

He left home at a young age to become a surfer. A boy who was told he would never read or write ended up going to college to become a chiropractor. Now, a professional philosopher and master of human development, his life is devoted to traveling the world to help people heal and live better lives.

I pulled out my scissors and glue stick and ran to the closest Walmart to buy a huge sheet of poster paper. It was time to create my vision board.

After hours of creative inspiration, my vision board was a completed masterpiece. Amongst the photos and symbols was a detailed story about the impact I will have helping people realize their greatness. There were images of influential people I admire in the world and descriptions of how I will work alongside them to create change and transformation on a global level. The creation of this vision board, in early January, set in motion powerful forces that manifested into reality.

I have been an admirer of Dr. John Demartini and his work for several years. I've read his books, experienced his methodology through another mentor, and sat in the audience during one of his inspiring speeches. I have rarely witnessed someone speak as passionately as he does about his life's work. A modern day philosopher and educator, he has written over 40 books and has been published in 28 different languages.

It was April 2nd and an email arrived to notify me that Dr. Demartini was in town to speak. I immediately bought my tickets for later that evening and prepared myself mentally to approach him and enroll him to be a Stranger. The time flew past and I soon found myself watching people line up to shake his hand, offer thanks, or to get a book signed. I lingered in the back of the room pacing back and forth. The crowd dissipated and I slowly made my way towards him. I spotted an opportunity and dove in, extending my hand. He made eye contact with me and was preparing to offer me a greeting when an enthusiastic woman jumped in front of me, blocking me out while she requested an autograph from John while waving a copy of his latest book at him. Like a skilled aircraft pilot, I quickly turned, banked with the wind, and retreated around the corner to avoid the awkwardness.

My mouth became unbearably dry as I waited, so I finagled a piece of gum from my wife to stimulate my salivary glands. She offered me a few words of encouragement while I internally debated my return. But, this interview had to be done. Confident, at least, that my breath was fresh, I bravely marched around the corner to face Dr. Demartini. He stood alone. I made my pitch, quickly explaining 52 People, and asked if he'd be Stranger 13. I waited for his response…

"Tonight?" he asked.

"If you can," I replied, waiting as time seemed suspended.

"Sure. Give me a few minutes and I'll come get you."

Thirteen weeks ago I started this little idea called 52 people, and now here I was, waiting to interview a man who has inspired millions of people worldwide, and who occupies a spot on my vision board.

1) What is your dream job?

"Well, my dream job is what I'm doing. I love researching, writing, traveling, and teaching. I love stepping foot inside countries around the world. I love inspiring people – helping them recognize their magnificence and helping them see they are really here to live extraordinary and amazing lives. I love watching people's lives change in front of me. It's one of the most inspiring things I know I can do and I can't wait to get up in the morning to do that."

2) What fulfills you?

"The same thing. I presented 426 speeches in 2007, 402 speeches in 2008 – I'm not sure if this year is going to break the 400 mark, but close to it. I'm working on a series of books and researching every day and that's what I'm getting ready to do when I get back to the hotel tonight. 'This man (Dr. Bruce Hoffman) has known me for 9 years?' (pointing to the gentleman standing beside him). He is a scholar in his own right and a great healer and as he would tell you. I pretty well do this every day and it is what I love doing."

3) What is your greatest fear?

"Greatest fear? Structuring, managing, and organizing the vast vision that I see for the work that I'm doing across the world. Delegating, organizing, and putting that together – the entire infrastructure of my vision. Probably the greatest challenge that I face is putting that infrastructure together."

4) What do you want more of in your life?

"Just a continuance of what I do. I just love doing what I do. I made a commitment when I was 17 to step foot inside every country on the face of the earth. I haven't hit every country yet – I'm still working on that. And, every time I get to speak in new countries, I'm inspired by that. We have some new people in Russia, Romania, Peru, and in Nigeria – so there are new countries every year and that's this year. So, I want to add at least four, five, or six new countries, at least, a year and I've made a commitment to go to every country."

5a) What is your greatest accomplishment?

"My greatest accomplishment is creating the Demartini Method®, which is a methodology that helps people see the hidden order in their daily chaos and helps them resolve conflicts and become grateful and loving and inspired and present and certain in their life. And, me having the opportunity to utilize this method to overcome the concerns that I've had in my life, including learning problems and doing what I love doing. So, my greatest accomplishment is me living my dreams and developing a method that can serve people around the world."

5b) What are you most ashamed of?

"You know you're asking a question that has little meaning to me. I don't have anything I'm ashamed about. The Demartini Method® makes you go back and look at your life and see everything as part of a magnificence. So, I don't have anything I regret and I don't live with shame."

6) What makes you sad?

"Well, if I set up an unrealistic expectation of myself or others and then don't have that expectation fulfilled, then I set up a momentary sadness and the purpose of the sadness is to make sure I set realistic expectations. And, I appreciate that. So, if I do experience a moment of sadness, which is very rare, I utilize that to give me feedback to set realistic expectations and thank my physiology for revealing that illusion and get on with it. So, I don't live in sadness. If I have a moment of it, I immediately use it to my advantage."

7) What is the hardest thing you have ever had to experience?

"Probably when I had strychnine poisoning when I was 17 and I was laying face down on the tent, vomiting, urinating, defecating on the tent, and lying there unconscious and having spasms that took 12 years to get rid of. That was probably the hardest challenge, particularly at that moment. And then a few other momentary challenges, such as... being shot at while running down a river bank in the mud and the muck, and then being nearly stabbed by two men when I was a teenager at 14 while hitchhiking through Mexico. I've had a few close calls with my life – nearly drowning while surfing in giant waves – but, those are probably the scariest moments. I mean, there are probably other ones, but those are the biggies."

8) What's great about you?

"What's great about me is that I exemplify what's possible for a human being if they set their mind to doing what they really love to do. And, I believe that there's a genius inside of me that is coming out and revealing itself and giving permission for other people to honor the genius they have inside them. And I think, me getting to live in this way is a service to the world. So, I honor and love that."

9) Who are you?

"That's a good question. On a metaphysical level, I'm possibly a cosmic particle of light – a soul that's manifested in a physical structure. From a physics perspective, I'm a form of energy matter. I guess from a social perspective, I'm 'Dr. John Demartini' traveling around the world as a teacher, healer, and philosopher. So, it depends on what perspective you look at me. Possibly, I'm a being that is manifesting an experience of love in an infinite variety of forms for eternity."

10) What question do you want me to ask you now?

"Whatever it is that would inspire you. What would be inspiring to you to ask?"

What is the one thing that got you to where you are now?

"Keeping record of the vast collection of experiences that I am grateful for on a nightly and daily basis. I was born on Thanksgiving day and when I was four, my mother told me to count my blessings because those who are grateful for what they've got experience more to be grateful for. So, I make it a point to document the things I am grateful for every single day. And, I've got probably the largest collection of experiences I am grateful for than anybody I've ever met. And, I think that's probably the most significant thing that I think a person could do in their life to live a full life. Because, as Henry James said, 'Nothing of the senses will ever satisfy the soul. The only thing that satisfies the soul is thank you, I love you.' And, if you can't say 'thank you, I love you' to yourself each day and the people around you and to your life itself, you're missing out on life. So, I think that's one of the wisest actions I know to do. That's my life – that's what I do. I document and keep it and it's all in my giant State of The Mission book."

It was a cold December day when I invested hours carefully choosing images that would be combined to create the mosaic of my vision board. My whole being was immersed in creating my future life on paper. There was passion in the story I created for myself as I placed images and wrote my story on the board. Once complete, I proudly hung my vision board up on my wall to connect with each morning. My life's intention was clearly and passionately born. Who would have thought that so many things would arrive so quickly?

Your intention is your invention. Make the choice to set your intention and fuel your growth with the energetic forces that help create your experiences. It is the direction you move in – you create your intention and then it sets you on your course.

Invent the direction your life will follow, cast the sails to your dreams by clarifying your vision and intentions, and stand back to witness the sails of life explode with the fullness of the energy around you.

STRANGER 14

"There were so many fewer questions when stars were still just the holes to heaven..."
- Jack Johnson

Sitting, waiting, and watching, she was alone. She searched for company – waited for a companion. She drank alone. She was thirty-one years old and still in school. She waited for the weekends, when she could reconnect with the bottle to disconnect from life.

My wife and I rushed home from a peaceful two night stay away from the city. We quickly cleaned ourselves up and drove over to hang out at a baby shower. Friends and family gathered together to honor the new baby boy who would grace the world with his presence in the next few weeks. It was a few enjoyable hours of gifts, finger food, and catching up with old friends before we had to rush out of there and on to the next engagement. My next stop – to meet up with the rest of the group from a bachelor party which had begun earlier in the day.

I arrived home, changed my clothes, grabbed my pocket recorder, and went to a karaoke bar to meet the group of guys. Not knowing what to expect on this evening, I was certain I was going to find Stranger number 14.

There she was, sitting alone at the bar. Her large brown eyes quickly scanned the half empty room before slowly descending onto her glass filled with vodka and coke. Pushing her long black hair behind her ear, she sipped her drink before making small talk with the bartender. Briefly glancing at the large screen displaying the hockey game, she appeared uninterested. The cycle started all over again as she scanned the room.

Other than our party, the place was maybe half full. It was still early, about 7:30, and the group of guys was relatively tame, so I figured now was probably the best time to make the move. I slid away from the table unnoticed and approached the young woman. Pocket recorder in hand, I walked up and took temporary residence on the stool next to her. I introduced myself and made a bit of small talk with her before explaining the meaning behind 52 People. Putting on my best charm, I asked her to be Stranger 14. She put on a furrowed brow and grimaced at the thought of being interviewed. She fell silent for a short period before I repeated my request. Staring off into space, she finally nodded in agreement. Stranger 14 was a 31-year-old business administration student.

1) What is your dream job?

"Owning my own bar because I spend enough time in there – I'd know how to run one."

2) What fulfills you?

"Friends and family – just being with them, laughing. I don't know, just like having good friends, having good company, and good times."

3) What is your greatest fear?

"Snakes. They fucking move man! Like they don't have legs and they move and they jump and ewww!"

4) What do you want more of in your life?

"Shit, I want more booze. Because, booze is good. Yup, I never go out too too much, so going out, it's like, being single and just going out now, it's like – yeah, I was missing out on a lot."

5 a) What is your greatest accomplishment?

"My purse collection – that is, yes. It's gorgeous, and it's all different designers and it's very expensive and I love them. I name them: Chanel, Betsy, Gorgeous, and Louis – you know Louis Vuitton."

5b) What are you most ashamed of?

"How easy I 'put out'. Because, I shouldn't. I should, you know, wait until like the second date or something."

6) What makes you sad?

"I don't know, everything – sad movies and shit. I don't know, I just watched 'Bridge to Tarabithia' and that shit destroyed me. I was like, a baby."

7) What is the most difficult thing you've ever experienced?

"A black eye. He was hard. That's why it was like, wow! Ouch. Not fun."

8)What is great about you?

"I'm fun. I'm just wild, crazy, and I'm a good time. I don't know. I don't know how to talk about myself."

9) Who are you?

"Who am I? God, these are the most random questions ever! I don't know. I'm a student. I go to school four times a week because I don't have class on Mondays. On the weekends I just go and get shit faced. I'm fun. Real – just down to earth real, like there is no bullshit. Pretentious – nothing shocks me. How many questions are there?"

10) What question do you want me to ask you now?

"When are these questions going to be over? I don't know. You are making me think and we are in a bar! Seriously, I suck at this. I don't know. What do I want you to ask me? If I would like another drink."

Would you like another drink?

"There you go!"

I bought Stranger 14 her drink and returned to the "Table of Testosterone" where the soon-to-be groom sat hunched over a wall of shot glasses. While I joined the celebration of his ensuing marriage, Stranger 14's answers lingered inside my head. I scanned the rest of the bar, observing the conversations around me and wondering how many of these people would willingly dive below safe, surface conversation.

I must admit, many times I have avoided large gatherings in the past simply to avoid surface conversations. I feel frustrated when every conversation is the same. The people could be substituted in any situation. The dialogue felt scripted. We were like actors rehearsing the same lines over and over again.

"What have you been up to? Married yet? What do you DO now?"

Here's the thing – I don't care what you do, I'm more interested in who you are.

It doesn't matter to me what you have. I want to know if you'll give it all away to be the person you truly want to be. Don't hide behind the words of a script. I want you to put down the papers and speak from your heart.

Galileo used the first telescope so he could peer deep into space to greater understand the stars and galaxy. If you desire to share your true self with others, you must put down your script and pick up your telescope. Look within. Discover, understand, and celebrate who you are. The telescope allows us to see things we are not able to see with the naked eye. Find your telescope. Next time you catch yourself in a scripted conversation – pull out your telescope. Become curious and experience the abundance of questions available when you see for yourself that the stars aren't just the holes to heaven.

STRANGER 15

"Death is not the greatest loss in life. The greatest loss is what dies inside us as we live."
- Norman Cousins

Usually someone who is well prepared in the face of adversity, she felt great pain as she sat and watched helplessly as a family member was battered openly in public.

I love the freedom that comes with working from home, but I can develop cabin fever slaving away all day in the same place I eat and sleep. My wife works in our office downstairs and I have transformed the dining room table into my place of creation. So, in service of keeping my brain fresh and activated, I made a commitment to get out of the house a few times a week and work somewhere else. My first non-home work location was Starbucks – great atmosphere, free internet, and great coffee. What more could I ask for? Oh, and did I mention, a possible site for a Stranger.

The pungent aroma of espresso penetrated my nostrils as the door swung open. I dropped my bag in a chair to claim my spot at a large study table and I ordered a coffee. Upon my return, a table companion set up shop just across from me. About forty years old, she had shoulder length blond hair and already had papers spread beside her computer. I placed my coffee down and took my seat. A combination of seat positioning and an obstructing light that hung in front of me prevented any direct eye contact between us.

We worked in front of each other for over three hours. The only communication between us was when she'd periodically step on the extension cord, momentarily knocking the power out on our table.

"Sorry," she exclaimed each time, appearing slightly embarrassed about her clumsy maneuver.

After a few hours of typing away, I had completed my work for the day and started to pack my stuff up. I slid the computer into my bag followed by my books. I contemplated whether or not to interview this stranger sitting in front of me. A familiar conversation took place inside my head.

Should I?

I don't know, I've been working all day and am a bit tired.

Back and forth this went, until reason chimed in.

The mere fact you are debating this tells me you should just do it!

Fine, I'll do it.

I leaned out from behind the light and tilted my head out of the glare so she could see me. I introduced myself with my most charming smile. She looked up, and her eyes had the red glassy tinge that develops after spending hours staring at a computer screen. She smiled and politely listened as I made my pitch.

In less than ten minutes I learned a lot about this mother of two, who runs her own business as a consultant for emergency services.

1) What is your dream job?

"That's a great question. A dream job for me – I don't necessarily have what it is, but I know what it would look like – just in terms of for me, it's a balance between my home and my work life is what I look for most. So, it's not necessarily the job itself. For me the requirements would be something that makes a difference in the broader community. So, it's not necessarily profit based – it's just something that makes a difference that way. It's something where I'm able to accommodate my family as much as I would accommodate a client or a work project. I think it's just a project where I leave at the end of the day and can feel like I've made a bigger difference beyond me and beyond the company."

2) What fulfills you?

"First and foremost, it would be my sons, the two of them. Work-wise, my fulfillment really comes quite simply from a client that would use me again. That's one of my biggest ones. And, just regular weekly, daily acknowledgment of a good job. It doesn't have to be anything profound – it's just a regular, 'Hey, great job'."

3) What's your greatest fear?

"Wow! Dying. Not being able to see all of the amazing things that I think are going to continue in this world – including my sons' lives. It's just, I think, every day has something different and unique to offer and to not be able to see that anymore is so disappointing to me."

4) What do you want more of in your life?

"More time for me as an individual – outside of my family, outside of my relationship with my husband. Just, if I could have anything, it's just more time for me as an individual – give back to myself. That was my big resolution – the only resolution for this year and I've done so very poorly at it. So, that's the big thing I'm looking at for this year. And, it's everything from as small as taking time to sit and have a coffee without working, to spending more time with my girlfriends, to learning something new – anything. New skills, a new area of life – anything. But, just time for me."

5 a) What is your greatest accomplishment?

"I guess the easy answer would be my family. It's obvious and it is the most beautiful thing I have accomplished. The scariest accomplishment for me has been starting my own business. It's been great and it's been scary and all of it."

5 b) What are you most ashamed of?

"That's a great question. I can't wait to read your blog to see what other people say now. I think I'm most ashamed, just in general terms, of not always living to be the type of person that I want to be. So, I have what I think are a pretty clear set of ethics and morals. Not that I've done anything incredibly morally wrong, but just more the type of person that I set myself out to be, and want to be, and I think I am most ashamed at myself and disappoint myself when I don't live up to those (ethical) standards that I set for myself. But, that's when I just, I hate it."

6) What makes you sad?

"Very much in the way that we just talked about. Anytime that I shame myself or disappoint myself by not living up to those sort of (ethical) standards that I've set for myself I get very disappointed. I get very sad if I can't practice the patience that I tell myself to be important and true. If I can't practice the compassion that I believe is important and true. Those things (ethical standards) make me incredibly sad when I can't follow through with it. That's the greatest. It's disappointing to me and I think it's, whether (other) people see it or not, disappointing to them because I'm not giving them what I believe what they deserve either."

7) What is the hardest thing you have ever experienced?

"I feel so fortunate that I think anything hard that I've gone through, when I come out on the other side of it, I look back and I think it wasn't as hard as it seemed at the time because I learned so much from it. I think, really one of the hardest things for me has been – how do I say it without getting too trapped in the details?... Watching family members being questioned in terms of their abilities, their skills, their intelligence, in a public forum and not being able to stand up and defend them for a variety of reasons, and a variety of really good reasons. But just watching that happen to a family member has been one of the hardest things I've ever had to..."

Was it the helplessness?

"That's it! And, knowing that fundamentally that the person, that my family, this member has been a great member and has done a lot for the broader community and individuals and to see people take a little slice of what they see and use that as something as a negative when you know what the full story is behind it, but you have no power or ability to change that perception. That's probably been the toughest thing."

8) What is great about you?

"Well, how long do we have? That's a nice question to ask. I think it is my empathy for other people and situations. I think I am a truly caring person who is not looking for anything in exchange and not receiving anything in exchange in those situations where I give. Those would be my biggest ones – the empathy and the caring – and really I think if everybody did that the world would be a better place."

9) Who are you?

"Oh my gosh! I think I'm a woman trying to figure herself out again – meaning my roles are constantly changing, have changed, a lot over the years and I think I'm at a point where I'm just trying to figure out who I am in the new role. What does that look like? What are my...how do

I define success now in the jobs that I do? And what is ultimately most important in those jobs that I'm doing because they can't all be the same in level of importance all the time? So, I guess I'm just trying to figure out the mysteries in life – the mysteries as they change and how I fit into that big picture anymore."

It's safe to say that many people have a great fear of dying. The problem is, as William Wallace says when faced with being executed in the movie Braveheart, "Not every man lives."

We are born with an insatiable curiosity to learn and an unquenchable desire to dream big when we are small children. So why do so few fulfill their dreams and achieve the "impossible" life? We are all products of repetitious conditioning that teaches us that things are too hard, only the lucky get what they want, or that we just don't deserve it. Soon our dreams become fairytales instead of fruition.

As a result, many people spend their days making a living instead of making a life. Dreams slowly vanish down the drain at the expense of being responsible. Responsibility banishes dreams into the dungeon of despair where they can fester into resentment. It's in this dungeon where our gremlins work diligently and masterfully to package this resentment and project it onto others in our lives. "It's their fault!" the voice inside your head tells you. This is the cry of the failures, the ones who fear dying, because they live in regret. They live a life of wasted time.

Stranger 15 seems to be spending her days living. She embraces changing roles and is curious about the mysteries of life and how she fits into the big scheme of things. What I really loved about her response to the fear of dying an early death is that she fears she will not be able to see the amazing things that will *continue* in this world. The opportunity and beauty in every day is what she doesn't want to miss out on.

Do you fear death? Or do you fear life?

Do not live in regret. Do not let the inscription on your gravestone read: 'Died at 32, buried at 80.' Now is the time to live. The attics of heaven are too full of unrealized dreams and ambitions. Resurrect your dreams and create new ones. Live your life and do not let the light inside you burn out.

STRANGER 16

**"What is important to remember is that people are resilient, and
people do have the ability to build again."**
- Christine Anderson

*His greatest moment had arrived. After years of planning, hard work, and
many obstacles overcome, he had finally done it. He did something few
would even dream of undertaking. The elation would be fleeting as shortly
after the celebration had ended his foundation crumbled and he was left
standing out in the rain.*

I'm a serial book buyer.

In attempts to be more cost conscious, I purchased a library card a
few years ago. I gave it a fair shot, but, honestly, I have a hard time giving
books back after I've read them. I like to showcase them on my bookshelf
like beastly trophies fresh from the taxidermist. This drives Erin crazy. She
accepts that I'm a compulsive bookworm, she just wants me to reduce my
consumption and borrow instead of buy. As much as I tell her I'm going to
stop buying, I just can't stop myself from going to the local book haven
and returning home with the latest page turner. Erin has developed an
expert eye and is quick to notice when my reading queue grows by a few
inches.

"Did you get another book?" she asks, shaking her head as if she
already knows the answer.

"Yeah, but it's the last one for a while," I say, knowing I'm not
telling the truth.

Despite all of this, I found myself walking through the aisles of a
bookstore for the second time this week. Curiously scanning the
biographies, perusing through the self-help section, and stopping to read
the back cover of all the 'books with a buzz' became quite exhausting. I
decided to take a break to stroll around and locate a Stranger.

I spotted him immediately. Standing in the home and garden
section, he was casually flipping through a book. Dressed in jeans, he had a

rugged, charismatic, strong jawed look to him and a soft gentle voice that reverberated kindness.

1) What is your dream job?

"I don't know. Honestly, I don't know. I've been thinking about that lately and I really don't have a clue. Honestly, I've been batting around that question for the last year, so I just don't know. If I knew I'd pursue it, but I just don't have a clue."

2) What fulfills you?

"My animals I guess. I've got a farm just outside of town. I look after horses and we do dog rescue and stuff like that. It's the unconditional love I guess."

3) What is your greatest fear?

"Speaking in public. Oh yeah! I did it in university and I just died. I don't know. It's just completely exposing or something – it's tough."

4) What do you want more of?

"Time."

What would you do with it?

"Same thing I spend all my time with I guess. I don't know it's a tough one. What would I do with time if I had more time? I honestly don't know. I'd pretty much do exactly what I'm doing – I'd just do more of it."

5 a) What is your greatest accomplishment?

"I built a house from scratch. It was a big job. It was a massive undertaking. It took me years to do it. It was a lot of work. I was proud of it."

5 b) What are you most ashamed of?

"I really don't know. I guess, always, that you should be farther than you are. I always feel like I should have done more. I don't know. It's just every day you go to bed and you think 'I should have got more done' but it's all encompassing right."

6) What makes you sad?

"The news. I don't watch the news. It's almost just brutal. I mean even this morning I watched it and there was just a note on there about a thousand Somalians died this morning you know – and it's not really a big story you know. Nine – Eleven, how many people died? And, it's massive but it's every day and people just brush it off. So, it kind of makes me sad, so I don't watch the news."

7) What is the hardest thing you have ever experienced?

"Death. Family member, that's easy. Actually I was building that house and I kept saying, telling my Dad I was going to come back and visit and I just kept finishing the house and a couple years went by and it was gone – he was gone. So, that's it."

8) What is great about you?

"I'm happy – genuinely. I mean aside from the obvious (laughing) – no that's a joke. My sense of humor, there you go! I'm genuinely kind and I'm generous. Charming – no just joking."

9) Who are you?

"I'm an artist sitting in front of a sketch pad who doesn't know what to draw."

10) What question do you want me to ask you now?

"What happened to my house?"

What happened to your house?

"It burned down a couple months ago. I'm just trying to figure out a new design for it and start over."

––––––––––––

So far this experiment proved that people anywhere are not only willing to connect, they have incredible stories to share as well. It seems so simple that I can approach any random person in a bookstore and tell an amazing life story, like Stranger 16. In under ten minutes, I was able to experience the genuine kindness and happiness he expressed as he spoke. I could read it in his eyes, his words, and his mannerisms as he grasped the design book in his hands.

You may be wondering how his house burned down. Pigeons had found a spot to build a nest in the structure of the house and somehow this nest caught fire late one evening. Stranger 16 barely got his family out of the house. They now reside in a converted shop, just across from the remains of what used to be their home. The home Stranger 16 labored on for years, his pride and joy, was transformed into a pile of ashes. Here he stood before me, among the books, embarking on a fresh start.

The emotion really hit me when Stranger 16 told me about his whole experience of building the house from scratch, losing his Father along the way, the house burning down, and now, after it all, being an uninspired artist with an empty sketch pad. My tears were a delicate mixture of compassion and admiration – feeling the pain of his loss and admiring the power of his resilience.

This is what makes the difference in life between success and failure, recovery and resilience. Whenever we embark on big journeys, begin great challenges, and dedicate our lives to something with meaning, we experience pitfalls and obstacles. What differentiates those who fall by the wayside and those who experience success is the ability to recover. When all is lost, what do you do? Steep in anger and sorrow, or go back to the starting line and begin with step one? Do you dwell in setbacks or simply see them as switchbacks up the mountain that allow you to climb higher and see further?

Stranger 16 may feel like an artist who doesn't know what to draw in this moment, but he inspires people with a different art. An art that sometimes cannot be seen, but felt and experienced when in its presence. The art that inspires. The art that people follow. The kind of art that can leave a man in tears. The art that lies in the ability to stand up and build again after everything has been lost.

STRANGER 17

"We don't stop playing because we grow old; we grow old because we stop playing."
- George Bernard Shaw

The jungle was silent and the only sound was the high-pitched buzz of a nearby mosquito. He sat, machine gun in hand, fearful of what might happen next. His thoughts were soon interrupted by a thunderous chorus of gunfire. The memories are difficult for this Vietnam vet., As a sufferer of post traumatic stress disorder, he desires to get back into the game of life.

My scream echoed throughout the seemingly never-ending tube. Surrounded by complete darkness, I felt my speed pick up, faster and faster. In a matter of moments I was launched from my safe container and I soared wild and helpless through the sky. My legs spread and arms flailed searching for something to grab hold of, instead I fell straight down and with a thunderous splash hit the water and sunk far below the surface. Thrashing through the water, I eventually made my way to the sweet air.

The hot Jamaican sun greeted my face as I returned to the surface and the sounds of Jimmy Buffet played loudly in the background. I had just been launched into the ocean by a water slide at Margaritaville, on Hip Strip at Montego Bay.

It was hours before my friends' wedding and I was one of five guys who decided to take the groom and go play for a while at Margaritaville. We slid down slides, made human chains across floating trampolines, and had survivor style competitions between us. We were being kids.

Near the end of our games, we stood on the top deck of the establishment and had a refreshing drink, laughed at ourselves, and nursed wounds from the action of the day. An older man stood nearby us and spoke to me about how much fun it was watching the five of us frolic out in the oceanic playground.

"Looked like a lot of fun out there. You can't really do that when you're my age," he said.

I smiled an encouraging smile, made a quick reply, and continued conversing with the guys. A few minutes later I was approached by the same man, only this time he was shirtless. He had grey-white hair and a medium build.

"I may be 64 years old, but I'm gonna do it anyhow!" he exclaimed.

"I gotta see this," I said, as I walked with him over to the slide. "I'll be watching from up here."

Without hesitation he jumped into the slide and disappeared down the ominous declining dark tube of terror. I could hear him scream with joy as he was whipped around each turn before he was violently launched into the ocean. I watched and waited for him to resurface. He popped up and immediately looked up to me and waved a victorious wave.

I must interview this man.

1) What is your dream job?

"Oh goodness. Probably a pro athlete. I just really like athletics. I tried to play football, I tried to play soccer, and I was never very good, but I always wanted to be a professional athlete. Just the camaraderie of being on the team and enjoying the feeling of being in front of a crowd would be really incredible."

2) What fulfills you?

"My artwork probably. I'm an artist and I'm a retired doctor. Just creating. I really like creating, making beauty out of nothing. That really matters to me."

3) What is your greatest fear?

"Being disabled – being physically disabled. Or, let's say mentally disabled, because I am physically disabled. Well my mind is my link to the world. Being able to think and process and not being able to do that would be a real problem. I don't even take medications that dull my senses. I won't take Benedryl or anything like that because then I can't think clearly."

4) What do you want more of in your life?

"Love – just contact with more people."

5 a) What is your greatest accomplishment?

"Probably being a psychiatrist – education. Because, I was going to be an artist and in Vietnam I was exposed to medicine for the first time and realized that making people well and helping them experience life better was very important to me."

5 b) What are you most ashamed of?

"Not doing as much with my education as I should have. I should be writing books, I should be – I don't know – doing a lot more than I am. But I'm retired now so I'm not doing it at all."

6) What makes you sad?

"Loss in general. I'm a two war vet. I have PTSD (post traumatic stress disorder). I have lost way to many people – it makes me very sad even thinking about it."

7) What is the hardest thing you have ever experienced?

"Same thing – loss of people. Not things – my house burned down and it didn't matter – people."

8) What is great about you?

"Probably that I genuinely care for human beings. I really like people."

9) Who are you?

"I'm just me. That's an odd question. You know I'm a person who is very multi-faceted. I love beauty, art, human beings, anything that people do. Music is very important to me. I'm just a guy who happens to have a good education."

10) What question do you want me to ask you now?

"I'm not good at this. I don't have an answer to that one. You know, I'm here with my sisters. I've never vacationed with them before. I want them to have a great time and, I don't know."

'What would it take for you to have a great time?'

'Them having a great time."

All worn out, the group of us sat at a table near the door waiting for our transport back to the resort so we could prepare for the wedding. I felt a hand touch my shoulder and I turned to find Stranger 17 standing above me, thoughtfully smiling.

"You know, what I should have said was: play more. I wish I would have played more." He patted me on the shoulder, shook my hand then disappeared through the door and spilled onto the Jamaican Streets.

At what time in our lives do we have to stop playing and be more responsible? What does responsible mean? Who are we responsible for – others or ourselves? I remember growing up hearing the expression 'Act your age.'

How confusing was it when you would sit in class in grade 4 and Johnny is flipping through his hockey cards next to you with one finger stuck up his nose and on the other side of you Gregory is writing the fourth stanza in an eloquent poem. What age are they acting?

What exactly is the way a 32 year old man is supposed to act? I should probably find out. I can search relentlessly for a model or measuring stick for a 32.5 year old and remain confused as to what age I'm acting and frequently judge myself based on that measurement. What is the punishment for the crime of acting an age that is not your own. Who is responsible for making this rule?

I had a conversation with a tourist in Jamaica who had four kids and is in the process of adopting two more. Her dream job is to be a mother with a house full of kids. Her kids are her connection to the innocence and playfulness in the world. She loves being pregnant and being around children because it reminds her that life is about being awestruck and playful.

Our nature is to play. When we are truly in the moment of playing there are no boundaries, no threats, and no time. To play is to be present with life.

Stranger 17 started as a passive 64-year-old man suffering from bystander apathy at the playful scene around him. He was too old – he had to act his age. In a matter of moments, he shed the serpent skin of the old man and stepped into the mindset that defied chronological age. After being spit out of the mouth of the water slide, his body soared through the air. His spirit soared even higher as time stopped, age ceased to exist, and wounds of the past had disappeared. The moment was his to play.

STRANGER 18

"People are pretty much alike. It's only that our differences are more susceptible to definition than our similarities."
- Linda Ellerbee

He stood in line with anticipation as his peers got picked to join different teams. When would he get picked? As the last few players joined their squad he stood alone once again. Not because he was inferior in ability, but because he was "different".

The taxi driver honked the horn, alerting pedestrians to clear the way as he sped through a tiny alleyway. He sat in the front seat and navigated me and my friends quickly yet safely through the tight Jamaican streets. His tall conductor style hat hid the long dreadlocks tucked up inside, and white patches of hair stood out amongst the thick blackness of his beard.

While we sped around the corners en-route to our resort, our curiosity surrounding our driver grew. His deep, smooth, 'Barry White' voice captivated us with stories of his life, his religion, and his childhood. When he was a boy, the other children were forbidden to play with him. As a young adult, nobody would hire him. What is now a celebrated lifestyle was once a sentence to social inequality and ostracism. To be a Rastafarian was to be different.

We arrived back at our resort. While the others exited the taxi, I immediately hopped into the front seat. I told him the story about my blog and asked him if he'd be willing to be Stranger 18. He nodded coolly then pulled his taxi away with me still sitting there.

Where is he taking me?

He quickly parked the van nearby and guided me away to escape the heat. The relief from the hot sun was welcoming as we found refuge in the shade beneath a large palm tree. It was here we sat in a couple of plastic lawn chairs and spoke tourist to local, interviewer to interviewee, man to man. On this day I got a lesson on what a Rastafarian really is.

1) What is your dream job?

"I gotta think. My dream job would have to be when I am financially able to sustain myself, and be a volunteer to try and assist people who are less capable of helping themselves. My dream is to help people. No matter where they're from, no matter what walk of life you're from – it's just to help the less fortunate. In Jamaica or whether they're from another part of the world."

2) What fulfills you?

"By teaching people to live a holistic lifestyle. To live righteous no matter who you believe in: Jesus Christ, Allah, Buddha, Selassie or who ever is your god. Just be yourself, live naturally."

3) What is your greatest fear?

"Right now I think my greatest fear is the social ills that are in and around the world today. People who are not as educated or updated, as most of us are, with the different types of diseases there are around today that can just snap your life like that."

4) What do you want more of in your life?

"What I want more of or most of in my life is truth and rights and equality for all mankind."

5 a) What is your greatest accomplishment?

"Well, my financial status in life right now. Being able to sustain myself, be self-employed, not working with a boss of someone bossing me around telling me what to do, when to do. I set my own pace, work when I want, and I enjoy my job – meeting people from all different countries, all different walks of life."

5 b) What are you most ashamed of?

"Well, when I look at my people, not being able to live of the certain standard. Living below the poverty line. People that are unable to find food, clothing, and shelter."

6) What makes you sad?

"Well being sad is really a state of mind when I look at it. Because no matter what it is I can find solace even when you think you are trying to get me down. I can make myself happy. Because I tell myself: 'I'm not gonna let you get me down or anything get me down.' So, sometimes it is just being unable to motivate yourself that makes you unhappy or makes you sad. I tell myself, no matter what it is, I'm going to tell myself that I'm happy. You can't make me sad. Because, when you think, or anyone think, that they are trying to do me evil or do me bad, that they are trying to make me sad, or in any way unhappy – that's when I am motivated. So, sadness to me is really a state of mind and I have learned to conquer that."

7) What is the hardest thing you have ever experienced?

"The hardest thing I've had to experience was when I started out as a Rastafarian. Having to deal with people, who were unintelligent people, that were not as forgiving as people are today or, for want of a better term, than people who are not as open minded as people are today about my lifestyle as a Rastafarian. People who did not see you for what you really were or what I really was, and then they look on you with the scorn. But now I see people everywhere I go. Mostly everyone I meet. They want to take pictures of me. They want to hear something from me. They want to learn from me. They like my hat. They like my hairstyle. They like the way I talk. You know everything I do it's like I'm a celebrity."

8) What is great about you?

"What I see that is great about me is that I've learned more about life the more I live. I understand people and that's the greatest education you can have – when you learn to really understand people."

9) Who are you?

"I'm a man of creation. Living the life that I am leading now, I try to reach out to the original patriarchs that we learned of or we read of in the Bible. I live as close as I possibly can to ancient fathers, our ancestors, that we learned of that has molded Biblical history. Because, no matter where you go no matter what you do the bible is the greatest handbook that any man or anyone can have. So, I try to be as close as possible with my forefathers. That makes me."

10) What question do you want me to ask you now?

"Well what I would like you to ask me is what you think of me. You tell me what you think I have told you – what you think I have said."

There is a great book written by the Arbinger Institute titled 'The Anatomy of Peace.' In this book it describes how the root of violence stems from the individual decision to see our fellow humans as objects instead of beings. My doctor, my ex-wife, gang member, Anglican – we live surrounded by labels. It is easier to persecute a label than it is a fellow human.

Early in our lives, we learn the ability to compare and contrast. As we age, we tend to push away comparison and allow contrasting to take over. What is it about making ourselves completely different from others that is so important? How do we honor our uniqueness while being tolerant of our differences?

Humans are labeled the same way cans of food are labeled. People may as well move about their days with tags on their shirts that spell out occupation, nationality, religion, sexual orientation, etc – this way it's easy to organize and generalize so we can stack people in groups like fresh produce lumped together at the grocery store.

Food offers us many things: different textures, different shells, different sizes, different qualities. It can also be deceptive. The prickly exterior of a pineapple bears a sweet fruit inside, while the small soft Brussels sprout delivers a bitter blow to the pallet. Despite the uniqueness, all food serves the same purpose: to nourish us – provide the body with energy and nutrients to keep it functioning. Each item may offer different things, but they all work towards the same common goal of fueling our bodies.

People have their many differences too. Different colors, different shapes, different jobs, some are sweet and some are sour. Despite the different labels people are similar.

Back to the question he asked me. What do I think of Stranger 18? I think, although he may appear different from me, we are very much the same. We both share a desire to help people regardless of lifestyle, faith, or location. We both have fears, however large or small they may seem. The experiences of our lives, although different, have shaped both of us into who we are today. We both have wounds from the past and will endure tests in the future. We may have different jobs but both of our vocations connect us with people. He may have a different wrapper, but we're both food. He may be packaged with dreadlocks and dark skin and may carry a different label, but ultimately, we are both here to learn about and contribute to the nourishment of ourselves and the people around us. We are each an ingredient in a massive recipe – each a part of a collective choice to make our lives and the lives of others more inspired, authentic, and fulfilling.

STRANGER 19

"The sunlight flashes off your windshield, and when I look up into the small, posted mirror, I watch you diminish – my echo, my twin – and vanish around a curve in this whip of a road we can't help traveling together."
- William Collins

She left her island a long time ago. At a time when she was ready to settle down, she picked up her family and sailed across the ocean. Having no work, she and her husband took a chance. They took a risk that this would give their children a better life and new opportunities.

I met my twin, and she arrived as an 81 year-old woman.

Working once again in my alternate office, a local Starbucks that I frequently set up shop in, I had my latest book purchase lying flat on the table, next to my computer. For the longest time, I have been waiting for this particular book, and on this day I was ecstatic to find the in-store computer screen reveal that it was finally in stock. Only one copy remained. I quickly ran to the section and searched. It wasn't there. How could this happen? I had been waiting so long for a copy to arrive and someone else snatched it from me. Refusing to surrender, I approached an employee for assistance.

"Oh, it must still be in the boxes in the back. It's not on the shelf yet," she said, staring blankly into the computer screen. Her words were those of an angel. This gave me hope.

She disappeared through the doors empty handed. I imagined the gruesome sound of boxes tearing and tape snapping as she courageously fought through the mess. She soon reappeared clutching the book, waving it victoriously through the air, before gently handing it to me in a way that said, "Just another day at the office."

Back at my table typing away, an elderly woman, coffee in hand, walked up and looked at my book. Her voice revealed a soft British accent as she told me how interesting my new book was to her. She wore a tricolor jacket and had a hearing aid in her left ear. Uninvited, she pulled up a chair and sat across from me. Enjoying the surprise company, I proudly told her about the book and the story of acquiring it. This led to a conversation about several other books, some of which we've both read. While I spoke, I noticed how she would stare at my lips and move her mouth, focusing on each word that would exit my mouth.

I could not pass up the opportunity to interview her. I made my pitch.

She agreed to be interviewed, but with a caveat, "Okay, but if I don't want to answer them…"

"No problem, if you don't want to answer them, you don't have to. The interview can be completely anonymous, I won't write your name," I explained.

"Well, I wouldn't tell you my name."

"Ok, well, let's give this a shot."

1) What is your dream job?

"Remember, I don't work. I'm retired. My dream job would basically be to help people. That would be my dream job – for people to find their way in life. Life doesn't have to be hard and if people can know which way to go that to me is a great satisfaction."

2) What fulfills you?

"Helping people – helping people, if I can. But, if they don't need the help I won't give it. Like, I won't try and force it out of them because I look at it this way. You have your journey and I have mine and if I can help you along your journey which makes it easier then I will do it. But, if you don't want the help I won't give it because life is a journey and people don't realize that. And people also don't realize that what you give out you get back. It's the law of the universe: cause and effect. Your journey can be a lot easier so why are you beating yourself up and blaming everyone else for what goes wrong? So, step back and see what it is you want to change and the universe will help you with it."

3) What is your greatest fear?

"I don't know if I have anymore fears. Sometimes I do, and I think that my greatest fear is not being able to take care of myself because, I see too many older people, they are struggling with life, they are struggling financially – I don't want that. Society in this day and age, we are a 'Me' society – 'Me and I'. And, they basically don't care about you or I as long as they have got what they want. But, they don't realize that somewhere along the line you're going to be where I am. So, that's my…it's being alone and not having anybody with me to cope with my situations when I get older."

4) What do you want more of in your life?

"More of people, more associations, less isolation because as you get older, well I see it, you know when you are older the less people want to have to do with you. And I don't know if they are scared, but one day they will be there. But, I've noticed if you go into the malls and other places like that and you see older people sitting, all you have to do is say hello to them and their faces light up because somebody has recognized them. It's the recognition that says, 'yah, I know your there.' But, people don't do that. It's like what I said: 'we are a Me and I society.'"

5 a) What is your greatest accomplishment?

"I don't know, I've had many. My greatest accomplishment is immigrating to Canada because it was very, very difficult. And, when I see my two sons and how they have made their lives is a great satisfaction. If we had stayed where we were they wouldn't be where they are. It was a sacrifice but also an accomplishment. We had no jobs and had two boys so it was a struggle."

5 b) What are you most ashamed of?

"I don't know, I really really don't. I can look back. But, I was going to say I gave my dog away, but I wasn't ashamed of that because she went to a very good home."

6) What makes you sad?

"Again I'm going to people. The way people treat other people. There is no compassion, no empathy. There is no feelings. People kill just for, maybe for, the fun of it. And they don't respect the earth, you know there's no respect for human life, there's no respect for animal life. People have to realize that the kinder you are it will come back eventually. You know it is what you give out you get back and people don't realize that. It is what you give that you get back. I'd like to see that change."

7) What is the hardest thing you have ever experienced?

"When my husband died and when my son was run over by a CAT, you know those big machines. Those were my hardest experiences. What I had to learn in this lifetime was abandonment. So, when my husband died I felt abandoned. My son is fine now, he's doing very well. He survived, but that was a tragedy. His was the first tragedy and then three months later that was when my husband died. How did I cope with it? I coped with it very well. But I was learning abandonment. Once you learn the lesson, I'm not saying they will go away, but they will come back to see if you learned it. They come back a little bit to see if you have learned this."

8) What is great about you?

"Me? I've learned to love myself – not quite, not a whole lot, but is being able to love myself so I can love the next person. You know, I can look at you and not look at you as a person but look at you as spirit. And, inside is beautiful and that is what I would like all people to have."

9) Who are you?

"Now what I'm going to say is nothing to do with religion, any religion, but I am in the image of God. That's who I am. And he works through me. And that's the only thing I can say."

10) What question do you want me to ask you now?

"Actually speaking, I don't know. I have to think about that one because you have asked the questions and I have answered them. What you haven't asked is… No, you have asked them all basically. I'm not going to say that I'm an open book because I'm a very reserved person."

The first thing that makes this stranger unique is that she picked me. It would have been interesting to observe our interview and the conversation that took place afterwards. She got on a roll talking about books, recommending books, speaking with the same excitement as I do when I share my reading adventures with others. Her mouth muttering the words as she read my lips, and my mouth open in awe as she told me stories or reflected back to me my own feelings or life lessons. In many ways she was my twin.

I have spent an awful lot of time the last few years being aware of my own abandonment baggage. So, when she spoke about her life lesson being abandonment, my stomach jolted and my jaw dropped. I felt like saying, "*Oh my god. Abandonment is mine too.*"

Historically, struggles in my relationships come back to the fear of abandonment. Don't get me wrong – I don't sit in the fetal position each day and worry, but the abandonment shows up with no rhyme or reason and it shows up in many forms. My responses are quite child like: detachment, anger, whininess. All of this fearing the possibility that my wife might find someone better, she might parish in a freakish accident, anything that would leave me living my journey completely alone. Who will I be if I am left all alone? If I don't have my wife, my family, my friends, if I was completely abandoned, who would I be?

Michel de Montaigne, of Solitude, writes: "The finest thing in the world is knowing how to belong to oneself."

Part of my journey is figuring out how to belong to myself. No one can teach it to me – it must be experienced. I guess even though my wife and family is with me, my journey is still a solo journey that is about uncovering the path of knowing how to belong to myself.

Stranger 19's words were the sunlight that flared off my windshield as our serendipitous encounter flashed before we both had parted ways. Separated by generations, we are joined as twins, souls echoing the sounds of life's lessons. As quickly as we come together, we vanish around the corner on this road we can't help but travel together.

STRANGER 20

"When I let go of what I am, I become what I might be"
- Lao Tzu

He could have stayed and done what everybody else does, but it didn't feel right. Despite the pressures to be the same, he left almost everything he owned and bought a one-way bus ticket out of town. Just barely a legal adult, he began a quest in search of something better.

The city was grey as the clouds hung low and the light rain threatened to turn to snow. I was dressed up in layers: thermal underwear, rain pants, and shirts galore underneath my water repellant jacket. There was no way the weather was going to scare me away today.

I was on my way to coach a women's touch football team. I had left the house a few hours before practice so I could go searching for Stranger 20. The venue for this week: the Greyhound bus depot. I hadn't been to the bus depot in years. When I was fourteen years old my parents shipped me up to Northern Alberta during Christmas break to spend two weeks with a family friend and to work on a fur trapping line. It had been 19 years since I'd been back to the depot and it seemed to be completely unchanged almost two decades later.

I walked down the long stretch of seats, watching for someone to make eye contact with me. I can imagine it looked a little creepy. Like someone wearing a black hazmat suit, there I was dressed up in rain pants and a rain jacket walking up and down the walkway looking at every person in the depot. After a few rounds of the premises, I spotted a young man sitting alone near the end. He wore emerald green leather skateboarding shoes, a white fishing hat, and had a fortress of backpacks and a sleeping bag surrounding him. I made my move.

Stranger 20 was a young man who just celebrated his 18th birthday. Packing up all his belongings, he had left his home and embarked on his own journey in search of new beginnings.

1) What is your dream job?

"Probably just be a professional cook. A cook – yeah that's pretty much my dream right there. I just love cooking because it's so peaceful. And, all I do is cook, put stuff together and people eat it – you know, feed people."

2) What fulfills you?

"Pretty much cooking – just cooking pretty much fulfills me and that's it. My family, but there not with me right now. Just me I guess."

3) What is your greatest fear?

"Getting beat up by a bunch of people. Being helpless and not being able to do anything back."

4) What do you want more of in your life?

"More adventure, more things to do, more stories to tell about what I did in life and all that – just making something instead of staying home and expecting something to happen. Just going out there and making something happen."

5 a) What is your greatest accomplishment?

"Backpacking and leaving home and not knowing where I'm going to sleep tomorrow. Leaving home and that's it. Just not having to worry about my family and all the stuff you think about when your home – just by yourself and figuring out what you're going to do tomorrow and the day after."

5 b) What are you most ashamed of?

"Being nothing where I used to live at. Just, I don't know, people didn't know who I was and just not making a name for myself over there and that's it."

6) What makes you sad?

"Ex-girlfriends. I don't know, just getting to know them and just leaving them and not knowing what's going on."

7) What is the hardest thing you have ever experienced?

"Leaving all my friends and not taking care of them I guess – leaving all my friends and all of that back home. Just not seeing them, and plus some of them hate me and I can't fix that or nothing. Just being lost."

8) What is great about you?

"I can get up and do anything I want because I don't have any kids or anything. I can just leave. I'm just trying to change and starting to be more lively and jolly towards the world and all that kind of stuff."

9) Who are you?

"Let me see, I'm pretty much just a happy person and I'm adventurous I guess. I don't like being in one place in one time all the time. And, happy pretty much."

10) What question do you want me to ask you now?

"I don't know. What would I be doing if I was home?"

What would you be doing if you were at home?

"Nothing just be sitting at home – nothing changing and wouldn't be doing nothing. I'd just be sitting there wasting. That's why I wanted to leave."

Benjamin Franklin said, "The definition of insanity is doing the same things over and over and expecting different results."

How many people do you know who spend their days complaining about their circumstances, lamenting about the way their life could have been? There are many people out there who loath their situations, but have the inability to see that they hold the power to change. To change it first takes awareness to see that change is possible, then the courage to make it possible. You have to let go and jump into the game of uncertainty and many aren't willing to play that game.

It is easier to dream than to boldly commit to action, and it is easier to complain than to fix things. Why aren't more dreams realized and more problems fixed? People for the most part are unwilling to change. It's easier to point the blame on others as being oppressive, circumstances as unlucky, or the world as unfair.

Letting go of your self prescribed label of 'not good enough', 'unfairly treated', or 'too busy or responsible to pursue that' means that you have to be something else. What is this something else? Who is it? Might it be something great? Something you truly want?

It takes courage to see that you want something different – that you deserve more in life. It takes even more courage to yank yourself from the situation you feel stuck in and it takes tremendous strength to take that first step into uncertain territory. Everything is uncertain territory until it feels like home.

Every day is the opportunity to become who you might be. Let go of who you are, embrace the change that your heart desires, and let the person you are becoming lead you home to where your heart lives.

STRANGER 21

"When we were children, we used to think that when we were grown-up we would no longer be vulnerable. But to grow up is to accept vulnerability. To be alive is to be vulnerable."
- Madeleine L'Engle

He had almost lost everything. He had faced the consequences of his actions and was able to recover from his past. As an alcoholic, he feared the day he might break down and have another drink. One small sip could hold the power to completely destroy his life.

It was mayhem outside of the San Francisco International Airport. In town, the night before beginning a week long Co-active™ leadership retreat, I was searching for my hotel shuttle among a melee of other travelers and had no idea what I was doing. There were a few women standing next to me, looking as perplexed as me. I asked them if they knew how the shuttle system worked and they threw their arms up into the air expressing defeat. I continued on, dragging my bag along behind me as I tried to locate a sign that would give me some sort of information. Once I left the crowd of people, I found a spot where I could go over a plan in my head. First of all, why didn't I research how to get to the hotel from the airport? I stood there for a few minutes, contemplating whether or not I should call the hotel and ask for help. As I pondered this, my attention was drawn to an older man standing beside me. I thought I'd ask him if he knew anything.

"Excuse me, do you know how this all works?"

"I do. Did you call your hotel and let them know you need a ride?"

"No"

"Where are you going?"

I told him the name of my hotel.

"You're in luck. I'm going to the same place, and here comes the shuttle right now."

Like a kind of troop master, he took over. He directed me to load my bag and we got on the shuttle bus. How fortunate I was. Out of the hundreds of people waiting outside the airport doors, I had asked the right person for help.

While we rode together, I thought about asking him to be Stranger 21. But there were others on the shuttle and it might have been an uncomfortable situation, so instead we made small talk. After about a ten-minute ride we arrived at our hotel. I thanked him for his help and wished him a goodnight and we parted ways as I walked into the hotel lobby.

Checking in at the front desk went smoothly and I exited quickly to my room anticipating a hot shower before bed. As I wheeled my bag along the road, I passed by the same man who helped me catch the shuttle. We exchanged greetings once again and I continued on my way.

"Would you like to join me for dinner?" he called after me.

"Definitely," I replied. "I'll track you down in the restaurant after I drop my bags off."

Like close friends, we made dinner plans. It was a little late, but I was not going to pass up a dinner invitation from the man who was going to be Stranger 21.

1) What is your dream job?

"I think I'd like to work with great minds. I'd probably like to be an educator. Not that I'm capable of doing it, but I think that's what I'd like to do. Probably the intellectual level that you meet on, on a constant and daily basis. Your mind is always stimulated. Your students stimulated and you stimulate them. I wouldn't want to teach grammar school. Or, maybe high school –I think that's it. I never really enjoyed work when I was working even though I had jobs that I enjoyed."

2) What fulfills you?

"Well, probably personal relations – relationships with people and my hobbies. I like to fish, I like to travel, I like to keep doing things – that fulfills me."

3) What is your greatest fear?

"I don't have any. Losing my wife maybe, but that's probably the only thing I'm afraid of. Being without her. I'm not afraid of being alone, but I'm afraid of being without her. We've been married for 37 years, it's not eternity but it's a long time. If I lost her I don't know what would happen.

I was an alcoholic. I drank a lot and it started affecting my life and so I quit. I quit 21 years ago and I'm deathly afraid of alcohol now. Everyone says, 'well you haven't had a drink in 21 years, why don't you have a drink? Just one.' And I think about it. I'll think about it later on: why didn't you have a drink? And, it's so frightening that I'd go right back to where I was, immediately. And that's scary, really scary."

4) What do you want more of in life?

"Probably want more years of good health. I want to live another thirty years, but I'm starting fall apart now. I've got the will, but the body is starting to fall apart. I'd just like to have more time – continue to do what I do now, what I enjoy. Nothing specific, just my life is so good I'd like to continue it. I'm at the age where a lot people start to, you know, they just die of natural causes and I still feel like I'm young. But I'm not, you know. My friends are starting to die now and it's a terrible time in my life or, terrible time in anybody's life when you start feeling vulnerable."

5 a) What is your greatest accomplishment?

"I don't have any great accomplishments. No, I don't have any accomplishments. I don't leave a legacy. I don't have anything I'm proud of. My children, but I don't have anything I'd brag about."

5 b) What are you most ashamed of?

"My behavior in the past. How I've treated some people who didn't deserve to be treated the way they did – mostly around alcohol. And, I've made amends with them. That doesn't fix it. It makes it easier for me. It doesn't make it any easier for them. I'm ashamed of my behavior. There's not much of it, but enough that still gnaws at you."

6) What makes you sad?

"Oh cripes! There are a lot of things that make me sad. That is such a big question. How people are abused, how we abuse people, how we abuse entire races of people, how we allow them to die needlessly. World conditions just really upset me. I can't answer that – I can't pinpoint that."

7) What is the hardest thing you have ever experienced?

"My father dying. Just my father, you know. I was by his side when he died and he didn't need to die. I don't know, he had more time on earth and he just died. I was at his bedside and it was hard to say goodbye to him. In fact, I think, I pulled the plug. I told the doctors to give him more morphine and the doctor said it was going to accelerate his death and I said, 'he needs it, he needs to go.' The doctor allowed me to take his life, but he wasn't going to live. He was in such agony and wanted to die, and I did it to him."

8) What is great about you?

"Nothing special, not that I know of. I'm a good friend. I'm loyal, trustworthy and kind. And I've been instrumental in getting a lot of people to stop drinking, but you don't count that because that's just part of staying sober – so I don't get any points for that."

9) Who are you?

"This is a pretty tough quiz you know. Well I suspect that I'm not who I think I am at all. I'm just the average guy just trying to get through life and be nice. I don't have any special desires. I don't have any special talents. I've done nothing spectacular. I've been a lot of places, done a lot of things. But, compared to a lot of my friends, I'm an amateur at life. My friends, they probably don't know the truth about me you know. They might just see something superficial and I might not be the nice guy that they think I am."

10) What question do you want me to ask you now?

"Ask me what I'm going to do tomorrow."

What are you going to do tomorrow?

"I'm going to go home and see my wife that I haven't seen for 15 days and it's going to be a happy reunion. I'm going to see my dog, my new puppy dog. And that's going to be about it – that's what I'm going to do. And I'm probably going to mow my lawn."

For some reason, out of the hundreds of people waiting to get a ride I ended up standing next to Stranger 21 on the curb outside the busy San Francisco airport. Thirty minutes later, I was dining with the 73 year-old in a hotel restaurant as though it was planned. During our conversation he opened up the window into his soul and told me his stories about battling alcohol, leaving work as an engineer to fulfill a desire to work outdoors, and the preciousness of childhood friendships. My interview with Stranger 21 was the first time I had a stranger ask me questions about my life as well.

It wasn't an interview. It was a conversation of deep meaning. Both parties as open books – both of us vulnerable.

He stared around the empty restaurant as he spoke about aging, death, and vulnerability. His eyes showed appreciation for what he had but an uncomfortable fear for what lies ahead. What does lie ahead?

As we break down with age, we get slower, less flexible, more forgetful, more dependent on others, and we eventually die. The feeling of witnessing your body breakdown, your friends pass away, regrets of un-vanquished dreams – all of this can be scary to face.

We grow up as children wanting to be strong, like adults. We work hard striving to be the ones who aren't pierced by emotional arrows, who can't be taken down by the criticisms and hurtful actions of others. We think to be strong is to be impenetrable, but the strength is in surrender.

Our greatest moments are not how we kept emotions out, but when we opened our hearts and saw the pools of tears grow at the bottom of a compassionate eye. We don't reflect lovingly on the time we pushed others away. We remember when we held tightly in our arms a crying child. To break down the walls is to invite a celebration of life. The vulnerability of having an open heart invites other open hearts to join you in fully experiencing your life outside of the lonely walls we previously built around us.

Vulnerability is truth. Vulnerability is loving and receiving love.

The power in vulnerability is knowing what you're exposed to and still making the choice to dance around the fire undeterred by the fears.

Cry when you're sad, tell me when you're scared, show me when you're hurt, and hold me when you want to be held – when you do this, it gives me permission to do the same. This way we can share the feelings that we have felt and will both feel again, only next time we won't be doing it alone.

STRANGER 22

"And those of you who face your fears squarely and give up your patterns of belief, will walk on the sun."
- Quantum Leaps Lodge *(Golden, British Columbia)*

She stood facing it. Feeling the tremendous heat on her face, one thought traveled through her mind: "I have come too far to turn around now." Her first step was the hardest, but as momentum picked up, she felt what it was like to feel invincible. In this moment, her past experiences of being abused were a distant memory.

Our feet were unusually cold as we stood barefoot on the clay, astonished by what we just experienced.

My wife and I had planned to get away together for the weekend. I had purchased a package over Christmas for a two-night stay in a river side teepee, including a thrilling day of white water rafting in class 4 rapids on the Kicking Horse River in British Columbia. When we called to book our dates at the lodge, we also had the opportunity to join up with a group doing a fire walking ceremony. When offered that chance to participate, I didn't hesitate. "We'll do it!"

The hot embers of the fire glowed brilliantly in the darkness of the night. Like a flashing neon sign, they beckoned us to daringly take the courageous steps into the steel-melting inferno. Hand in hand, my wife and I defied the physical realm and with every step we felt coolness instead of heat, together we walked across the fire.

We stood in exhilaration among fifteen others who had just walked barefoot over the coals of a fire exceeding temperatures of 1000 degrees Fahrenheit. While part of the group celebrated on one end of the fire pit, I approached a woman who'd just experienced the excitement of her first fire walk. She was a mother in her late twenties, a musician, and Stranger 22.

1) What is your dream job?

"There's two. Can I have two? The first one would be running, living, on either a ranch or acreage with unlimited music and art resources and shipping people from all over the world who may have talent but not the resources to come stay with me for six weeks or two months and just be well and happy and dance and sing and paint. That's my big dream. My other dream is to be a very – got to word this properly – an internationally known musician without the celebrity. With no celebrity status, no VIP, nothing – just living in my ranch, but sharing music with millions of people."

2) What fulfills you?

"Dancing with my daughter. We spin. We laugh. We are heart to heart. I feel like she's still a little baby. We just have a connection that is very, very, very strong and that is the best way for us to show that to each other. She tucks herself into me. She is really long and she just tucks in and we just dance and I feel like I have her back as a part of me."

3) What is your greatest fear?

"Having really rotten last conversations with people. Like, the last time I ever talked to him (best friend). Because even though I believe we can correspond with the deceased, I don't want to have any physical regrets. I don't want to live every, and I don't often, live every conversation as if it's the last because that would be unhealthy for me to be thinking about that every time I talked to somebody. It's just important to say what is the best thing to uplift someone because it's just good. I think that is the thing I am most (afraid of) – that's about the top one."

4) What do you want more of in your life?

"Free time. I would sit with my daughter and read a book or do nothing."

5 a) What is your greatest accomplishment?

"My greatest accomplishment has been returning back to the thing I was supposed to be doing all along and achieving big things with it. And the second, What was the second part? Oh you haven't told me the second part yet (laughing)... I'm anticipating. We've had national recognition with our project and I'm thinking that it's a huge accomplishment for me who's come from kind of a self-defeating mentality. Actually, this is more to the truth: I have overcome myself and my own self-defeating activities and mental thoughts and (fire walking) is a part of it. This was huge. But, when I compare it to when I was – you know – a kid, like a teenager, this stuff I overcame it's been way bigger than this. So, as you fine tune things, get more focused and big. But, just becoming a positive person has been a huge accomplishment I think."

5 b) What are you most ashamed of?

"Allowing somebody to abuse me for years. And, living that out and taking it out on people that I love. That's the biggest thing – that's the biggest shame that I have."

6) What makes you sad?

"Losing time. Losing time with – it all comes back to – my daughter. Losing moments that I wish I could undo, that I compensate for, that I realize that she's smart enough to realize what I'm doing."

7) What is the hardest thing you've ever had to experience?

"The hardest thing I've ever to had experience was losing my best friend. The fact that he really, he really wasn't gone. And, everybody pretended that he was still here, but he's gone. Even though he's 'here', we've lost that person who was there. There were parts of what I found out after losing him that made me feel betrayed. So, just the inability to go back and have a conversation and say, 'what the hell was going on?'"

8) What is great about you?

"I get up – I get up again. I get up – You can't stop me. You push me down, I'm going to get back up. And I've learned to sort of roll with it and enjoy getting. You know what I mean? Just the rolling and the, I think, that I have a good outlook. I think that I uplift people and it's because of my experiences that I can sort of tap into where somebody's coming from and say you know, 'I know that fucking sucks, let's go this way.' So, it's kind of cool because I, I'm glad that I went through all that stuff so I can be somebody special to people."

9) Who are you?

"Who am I? She's the one that laughs very loudly, throws temper tantrums, writes important poetry, seeks out the one who is not happy and try to bring them up. She's full of energy. She's tapped into people. She suffers from self-imposed depression but bounces back with something better. And, she's a really good mom, a really good mom who's just going through some shit so that her daughter can be an even better mom.

10) What question do you want me to ask you now?

"How do I perceive our role here in the grand scheme of things?"

How do you perceive our role here in the grand scheme of things?

"I think… I know that we, we are continuous, we are continuous and unending life force that just is manifested in many different bodies and blades of grass. And I think, that we, if we had special glasses on we could see that everything is like sparkly and energy. And that we can call on God, or Buddha, or Allah, or whoever because it doesn't matter because it's all the same, it's all the same like vehicle or source. So, I think that we as people are individually extremely powerful and we have the ability to do anything if we are, if we are able to focus on our own connection to the fill in the blank. And, it is very powerful to be – to have contrast and negativity and allowing it to shoot out good stuff and wants and desires and just we that we are embracing life. We are here to laugh and love and live and cry. We're just here to enjoy, you know."

––––––––––––––––

Prior to walking on the fire, the participants all took part in a process of passing the wood. We lined up and handed the pieces one by one to the next person in line until it was all placed on top of the pile. The process was a practice, an opportunity to become familiar with the wood and to honor the transformation it was about to go through in service of our individual transformation. How can one walk on the extreme temperatures of the fiery red coals without burning themselves?

The whole process was built into a four-hour ceremony in which we built up the mind and conjured up the courage to let go of our limiting beliefs. We were guided to obtain a mental focus where our energy could match the energy of the fire. The belief is that once this happens the fire could not burn our feet. By making the choice to do this, there was no room for self defeat – absolutely no chance to face the heat with any mental roadblocks.

The fire is a metaphor for those daunting challenges that lie on the path in front of us. The glowing cinders are indicators of the fierce power that faces us head on. When faced with these challenges we can choose to react in several ways. The patterns ingrained into our heads from childhood warn us of the severity of the heat and the pending physical damage we dare to face it. Many times, we temporarily cease these beliefs and step courageously towards the fire, then pull back from the heat at the last minute as fear grabs hold of us.

We must let go of our limiting beliefs and stop trying to rationalize or make sense of things and instead hold on to the innate wisdom that resonates inside of us. When we do this, we shine as bright as the fire. We glow. We defy logic and match the energy of the fires we encounter. This gives life to the fire inside of us – the internal fire that pushes us past our former boundaries, the raging fire that lives within us that when acted upon inspires others to walk on the sun.

STRANGER 23

"Would you tell me, please, which way I ought to go from here?'
'That depends a good deal on where you want to get to,' said the Cat.
'I don't much care where ...' said Alice.
'Then it doesn't matter which way you go,' said the Cat.
'... so long as I get somewhere,' Alice added as an explanation."
- Lewis Caroll

While most people her age gear up for a leisurely life of retirement, she was doing something different. A tumbleweed of sorts, she didn't know where she was going, but she knew what she wanted. She didn't know what she would receive, but she knew what she would do. Whatever happened she would be free.

I held a coffee in my left hand while I attempted to hold a stack of twelve books under my right arm. Even though I struggled to maneuver, I continued to root through piles of books to unearth more gems for our personal library. As I added another one under my arm the pile slowly bowed before exploding across the floor. I quickly, but carefully, set down my coffee and scrambled to pick them up as crowds of people dodged me and the mess I had created.

Most people had brought a large bag or box with them. Unlike me, they we're veterans of the book sale. This was my first, and my lack of experience was apparent as I foolishly struggled to manage my books while refusing to relinquish my hazelnut latte.

A kind gentle soul, a volunteer at the book sale, witnessed my feeble balancing act before she placed an empty box in front of my face.

"This should help," she said with a smile.

"Thank you," I said as I flashed a helpless grin back at her.

My wife and I fared pretty well at the sale. We filled up the box, plus another bag we borrowed, and dumped the first shipment into the trunk of the car before returning for round two. At the end of it all, we purchased 45 books for just over $60. While a mass of people continued to rummage through the piles of books, I started my expedition for Stranger 23.

A man sat alone on a picnic table with a box of books on his lap. The box was filled with fantasy books adorned with dragons and warriors on the covers. I approached him and made my pitch. As if protecting a chest of gold, he held his box tight to his body as he suspiciously watched me. "Not interested." He shook his head and looked away.

Continuing on, I strolled around the perimeter and was about to give up when I spotted the same woman who had saved me earlier by providing me with a cardboard box. "They let you have breaks here?" I joked. She laughed and nodded. Undeterred from the previous rejection, I made my pitch. With no hesitation, she became Stranger 23.

1) What is your dream job?

"Helping people find themselves. Well, I look for my own spiritual path a lot and I'm open to whatever paths there are and I'd like to help people discover that for themselves."

2) What fulfills you?

"I guess it's related to question one – helping people. Helping people and learning about what makes life work."

3) What is your greatest fear?

"Not doing all the things that I want to in life. Well, I'm 66 so you know I'm nearing probably the other end of life and so there's lots of things I still want to accomplish and do: some more travel, seeing other places in the world, meeting other people in the world, finding out what people love."

4) What do you want more of in your life?

"Friendship. Friends and support are one of the things that makes life worthwhile."

5 a) What is your greatest accomplishment?

"Well, I suppose my studies. I have a Masters in Psychiatric Nursing and it's helped me along the way. And, I've been able to help lots of other people with it."

5 b) What are you most ashamed of?

"I guess not doing enough to help."

6) What makes you sad?

"Waste in the earth – the fact that we're not really conserving what we need to, to preserve Mother Earth."

7) What is the hardest thing you have ever experienced?

"I guess the death of my dad – just that his last few years were lost in dementia and so we couldn't really communicate."

8) What is great about you?

"I think the fact that I'm open to whatever. I'm really curious, interested, available to what's out there. I have a super sense of humor."

9) Who are you?

"I'm an individual who is aging, who has lots of things to learn, and is open to any new learning."

10) What question do you want me to ask you now?

"Where do I want to go from here?"

Where do you want to go from here?

"Any place the world will take me."

———————————

I tilted my head in contemplation when I thought, *How can you help someone discover their own path? Isn't the discovery of one's path an individual exploration? Doesn't 'help' automatically assume that it is not their own path?*

Look at the story of Alice in Wonderland and the conversation Alice had with the Cheshire Cat about where to go. The Cat helps her by asking questions only she knows the answer to. "Where do you want to go?" and "Then it doesn't matter where you go then does it?"

Alice responds by saying something like, "Well, wait! I want to go somewhere, just not here."

What happens in life when we know we want to go somewhere but don't know where to go? We feel stuck. Sometimes it feels like we are moving backwards, or in a completely different direction.

I was walking through a stone labyrinth for the first time a few weeks ago. Silently, step by step, lost in the presence of the moment, I walked through it. Sometimes it felt like I had made progress towards the centre, at other times I felt as if I was heading completely in the opposite direction. My mental chatter told me something wasn't quite right, but I just kept walking step by step. Round and round I went until finally my journey ceased in the center of the labyrinth. While standing in the center I understood the metaphorical significance of the labyrinth.

The journey can be deceiving. When you think you are on the right track you can suddenly end up facing the wrong way. As you get closer to your destination you may be led to believe you are moving back to the place you started from. The longer you stop, the more anxious you can become while wondering, waiting, thinking, figuring things out. It is only through patience, trust, and putting one foot in front of the other that you ultimately end up in the right place.

Kind of sounds a little bit like life.

Where does Stranger 23 intend to go? Any place the world will take her, just as long as she goes somewhere.

STRANGER 24

"The best things in life are unexpected – because there were no expectations."
- Eli Khamarov

He stood backstage as the crowd buzzed with anticipation. He had just laid down his best possible effort and now all that awaited him was the official judgment. A professional performer, he wondered if he would ever experience the feeling of being a champion.

The community centre was packed as I was attending a fundraiser for a relative of mine who was battling leukemia. Sitting at the back of the building with my friends and family, our eyes focused on the stage up front. The music blasted and the crowd anxiously awaited the performer to step out and start the show. The bright lights danced wildly as the sound of Strauss's 'Sprach Zarathustra' built into a powerful crescendo. At this moment the lights flickered and the smoke lifted and a man appeared on stage in his full-body black leathers and began to rock the house. The 50's-themed fundraiser was now complete with the arrival of "The King."

I have always had a strange connection to Elvis. Ever since I can remember, I was reminded that my birth date fell on the same date as Elvis Presley's. Because of this, I developed a habit, from a very young age, that any time I was asked when my birthday was I told them January 8th and added, "Same as Elvis". So, you can bet that I was not going to let an opportunity to interview my birthday buddy pass me by. Even if he was not the real deal, who gets the chance to interview Elvis?

My first attempt was at the completion of his first set. He exited through the side doors of the building – a perfect place for me to conduct the interview away from the noisy crowd. My strategy was to intercept him by taking another route and casually bump into him. When I rounded the corner, I spotted him. His tight black leather suit hugged the curves of his body while a cigarette dangled from his lips. Much to my chagrin, "The King" was surrounded by adoring fans, making it impossible for me to conduct the interview. With the crowd around him, I decided to go to Plan B, which consisted of going back inside and determining what to do next.

I thought I had lost my chance when I saw him return and go back on stage to prepare for his second set. But, the ghost of the real Elvis was shining down on me as the impersonator left the stage and walked passed me to use the washroom.

Almost falling out of my chair, I quickly darted behind him. I stopped him just as his outstretched hand touched the washroom door and I made my pitch. He agreed, but with a caveat. First, I had to let him finish his current task: using the restroom.

Stranger 24 was one of the top Elvis impersonators in the world and had been performing for almost 20 years.

1) What is your dream job?

"Well this job right here – not a question asked. It's not a job. It's not a job. When people go to work they work because they have to. I don't have to do this, but because it's so much fun, and even though it's work, it's not work as much as I enjoy it."

2) What fulfills you?

"The people – the people's desire to continue come out and watch the show where there's nothing new, and there hasn't been since 1977. And yet, some of the music is over 50 years old and they still love it. So that's very fulfilling for myself."

3) What is your greatest fear?

"Losing my voice on stage. It's happened before. I was actually doing a show in Carbon and I had a little love missile blow up in my voice box, and instant laryngitis. And, I mean so bad that I couldn't talk actually for about two weeks afterward and that's pretty scary. So I look after that pretty well now."

4) What do you want more of in life?

"Good question. I think probably the most important thing to me is family. There's nothing more important than family. My wife comes along and runs the lighting and does all of the things and makes all the suits and really has a tremendous heart. I've had my little grandson come out and sing with me and that's been wonderful. But, family – if you don't have family you don't have nothing."

5 a) What is your greatest accomplishment?

Winning Canadian National Title. Because, I wasn't supposed to win – so that made it exciting. Having longevity in this business, doing an Elvis when there is so many of them out there, I think, is very important to me. I want to go for a few more years – certainly want to perform as long as Elvis, for as long as Elvis performed living, which is 22 years. And, we have about four more years to go so we'll see what happens."

5 b) What are you most ashamed of?

"Splitting my pants in the middle of a finale – slid across the stage that was it, busted my seam right out of my pants that was the end of it. That was pretty embarrassing. And, I was in the middle of the song so I had to finish the song. Judged song right? So you got to finish it, right? That was pretty embarrassing."

6) What makes you sad?

"I think things like we're doing tonight for young people that don't really deserve to be as ill as they are – that hurts me. Children should have a life. They should have longevity. Unfortunately, in a lot of cases that doesn't happen, especially with the type of illness that we're trying to raise funds for tonight. Children's leukemia is a killer. Breast cancer is a killer. I mean, we don't want those type of things and until they find a cure for it, you know, maybe the gift that I have of selling Mr. Presley can raise enough money to help."

7) What is the hardest thing you have had to experience?

"I think the hardest thing I have ever experienced was almost losing my wife and youngest daughter at childbirth. She had about 25% chance to live and the little girl had 5% chance to live. And I thank the good Lord, and a for few prayers and so forth, that she's uh, she's doing very well. And, (my daughter's) a mother – she has two children. And, my wife is still alive and I'm very thankful to the good Lord for that. That's pretty tough."

8) What is great about you?

"I'm humble. I'm a humble person. I go and I just gig. And, lots of guys it goes to their head. And, that wasn't, that wasn't what we try to portray. Elvis was very humble, very religious person. And, even though I'm a little bit of showboat on stage, I still remain humble. I don't let it go to my head. No matter all the accomplishments that we've been able to do over the course of the years you have to remain true to yourself and if you don't do that then you have nothing."

9) Who are you?

"I'm Jim. That's who I am hard-and-cold. I pay tribute to Elvis Presley – that's what I do. That's basically the-hard-and-the-cold, very simple very straight-forward answer. I'm Jim. I'm not Elvis Presley – I never profess to be. And, hopefully, people enjoy what I do because it brings them back to a time when things were simple and they enjoyed life a lot more."

What stood out to me most in this conversation was the way he explained winning the Elvis impersonator National Championships and why it was his greatest accomplishment. "Because, I wasn't supposed to win – so that made it exciting."

I remember my greatest moments as an athlete – every one of them came when I wasn't focused on the outcome. The only thing I focused on was the process or the moment. There were no expectations dancing inside my head only the present moment to be completely immersed in. The most important element that propelled me to be one of the top drivers on the National Bobsleigh Team and that aided my growth through the system was this: having no expectations. I just stepped into the journey and worked at getting myself to get better and subsequently I climbed my way higher and higher.

I expected a certain degree of commitment from myself for my craft. A commitment of pouring myself into the effort was required in order to be my best. I soon lost myself in the process and developed what Tal Ben Shahan calls "arrival fallacy" – the belief that once I finally arrive at a destination, I will be happy.

I started making up a story that once I got to the Olympics I would be happier, be more valuable, more important. I began to live my life with my mind in the future and I validated myself based on that belief. As soon as my expectations shifted to the outcome and destination, I became imprisoned by self-criticism, judgment, and anguish. I let my excitement and curiosity about being an athlete fade away. As a result of my "arrival fallacy", my best results were followed by crashes or extremely poor finishes.

What would have been possible if I had let go of my expectations and held onto what I could control? What if the only thing I held on to was my attitude and effort and I clung to that every day as I began my training? What would the rest of my life look like if I lived this way?

STRANGER 25

"The past is a foreign country; they do things differently there."
- Leslie Poles Hartley

Her past was filled with many mistakes, but her future remained bright. As a young single mother, she used her experiences not to hold her back but to push her forward.

Every time I go to the movies I do the same thing – I over-eat.

Movie theatre popcorn is so unbelievably irresistible for me that I can't leave even the largest bag unfinished. As if the popcorn and soda pop isn't enough, the combo I "need to get" throws in a large bag of peanut M&Ms. My mind plays a trick on me and convinces me these are all perishable items if not eaten in the hour-and-a-half after they're purchased.

Erin and I were attending a late afternoon screening of "The Hangover" to take in a slice of quirky, shock-value humor. The movie theatre concourse was getting quite full as patrons started lining up to get their tickets for the early evening show. People played video games, lined up for refreshments, or stood around waiting for friends to meet them. Erin dashed into the mall to pick something up, while I went on the prowl for Stranger 25 at the cinema.

As I scanned the crowd, I noticed a young woman texting on her phone and looking around as if searching for someone. I walked around the perimeter but kept getting drawn back to this young woman. I finally gave in to the internal urge telling me to approach her and make my pitch. I sauntered up and leaned in to get her attention. She stood up straight and shot me a look that was a mixture of surprise and caution. When I explained to her what I was doing, she laughed uncomfortably – not sure if I was serious or not. Despite her initial apprehension, this woman in her mid-to-late twenties agreed to the interview.

1) What is your dream job?

"Oh wow, absolute dream job? Owning my own book keeping company – not very exciting, but I can work from home and make my own hours and it's what I enjoy doing."

2) What fulfills you?

"Spending time with my son. Well, he's three years old. It's just, as he gets older he changes every time through each stage."

3) What is your greatest fear?

"Heights! I don't know, it's just too high for if I fall and hurt myself, you know like into a plane crash or, stuff like that. I had a traumatizing moment when I was like in Grade 2: someone pushed me off the top of a slide and I was really small so it was really high. So, I think that's why I'm scared of heights. Yah, it wasn't pleasant."

4) What do you want more of in life?

"Money. First of all, get myself financially set and just go with the flow. I don't know, just do whatever I want to do. Right?"

5 a) What is your greatest accomplishment?

"Getting my accounting diploma, so far. When my son was born I wanted to provide him a better life so I wanted to expand my education."

5 b) What are you most ashamed of?

"Nothing, nothing."

6) What makes you sad?

"Being lonely. Well, everyone around me is getting married or they have a spouse or something and they always seem so happy and I'm having a very difficult time filling that out."

7) What is the hardest thing you have ever experienced?

"Moving to another city. I had no friends out here. Starting all over again – just establishing my life all over again. For me, it was a big step because I moved away from most my family and all my friends and I had to start all over again here."

8) What is great about you?

"I think I'm an easy going person. I'm open-minded. I don't judge anyone. I'm pretty much happy all the time. I think my main thing is being open-minded because I'd be a huge hypocrite if I wasn't. Just from experiences from my past, I can't judge people because I would say I wasn't the greatest person in my past. But, being open-minded, being friendly, I'm willing to help everyone and willing to bend over backwards for my friends."

9) Who are you?

"Who am I? Oh that's funny...I don't know. As a person? I make you feel good about yourself. I'm always positive. I never think of the negative things and always try and cheer up that person."

I stand on the border of a nation and watch. I look across the median separating two nations and detail the experiences of the people from the country of Past. I am the only internal witness for the citizens of this nation, which grows with every passing second. The nation is one of complexity and change. Using historical reference and interpretation, this is what I can tell you about the country of Past as someone who has witnessed it from the inside:

Past is a country where the land is full of large obstacles that impede movement – a home of victimized people. Past is a place where adults must be stoic individuals who rarely show emotion in situations normally associated with pain or fear. This country has people who pass by each day refusing to open themselves up and show their inner truth for fear others won't like what they see.

The people in this country do things to impress others. They take on big dreams and tasks to gain the love and admiration of those around them. The people here conform to the group – making decisions on who they should be and what they should do even if it doesn't feel right.

The people of Past are great at assuming other's feelings and intentions. As a result they never ask, "Why?" These people think objects and achievements can influence others to love them. This country houses those who only talk about the weather, their jobs, and their cars when deep down inside they want comfort from their fears and support in their dreams. These people struggle to tell their friends and family "I love you." The people in this country are never wrong – it's always someone else's fault.

The people in Past have big ideas, but shrink back at the thought of stepping forward. The people in this country are consumed by the fear of failure – their minds are constantly exhausted by spending unnecessary energy on old mistakes or future unknowns. The people in this place have a deep desire to let their true colors shine through, but fear that by shining they will selfishly push others away. Refusing to appreciate their strengths and often lament about their weaknesses, the people here are critical of themselves. Leaning on the escape of numbed senses to open up and lose their inhibitions, the people of Past have many times slipped into the false solace provided by alcohol or drugs. Past is a country where men have to prove their masculinity by having to be better at sports, sleeping with different women, and proving their wealth through obtaining useless, expensive, shiny things. This is a country of men who want to ask for help but are afraid that by asking for support they are exposing a weakness.

This country is a war torn place where the fiercest battles have been waged. This country has spent excessive resources at war with Imagi-nation. The country of Past has assumed that it is an island nation, isolated from the rest of humanity, alone in their struggles.

I know the history of this country well. I have seen and experienced the battles and day-to-day life of Past. Although the details of this country are only read in the confidence of one man, my journal each morning holds the tribulations of a nation.

A nation so dear and close to me is yet foreign. The people have taught me valuable lessons and will continue to teach me. I have a place in my heart for the people of Past, but the people there do things differently.

STRANGER 26

"Nobody can go back and start a new beginning, but anyone can start today and make a new ending."
- Maria Robinson

He never thought it would happen. One poor decision changed his life. After a long night of partying with his co-workers, he made the decision to drive home. Never did it cross his mind that this decision would change his life.

The bag of dog food was completely empty and my young retriever-poodle cross had to eat. Although we had been generous in offering her little vegetarian snacks from the kitchen table, we weren't about to provide her a full meal of bananas, cucumbers and tomatoes (her favorites). So, off to the pet store we went.

The sun was hot as we drove to the closest location. As we pulled up into the parking lot, our attention was drawn to a fully inflated rubber dingy nestled perfectly in one of the parking stalls. A young man lazily stretched out inside of it, hands behind his head. Shirtless and basking in the sun, he casually watched traffic as he laid there looked half asleep.

We pulled in and parked about 4 stalls adjacent to him. My wife laughed at the randomness of the little boat as she left the car and ran into the pet store. I became curious and left the car and walked towards the young man. With my recorder in my pocket I approached him. "Did you paddle here?"

At the midpoint into the journey of 52 People, this interview took place on a boat – rather, a rubber dingy – resting on the pavement in a busy strip mall parking lot. Just me and a 20-year-old man on a hot summer day.

1) What is your dream job?

"Probably surfing and rock climbing or like teaching people how to do it. I have no idea. Probably living somewhere close to the ocean and having a good time all the time, I guess, would probably be my dream job."

2) What fulfills you?

"Just life in general man. Like, I'm happy every day coming to work. And, I lay in boats. Can't sweat the small stuff, I guess, is what I'm getting at. So, just happy to be alive. Every day is a good day basically."

3) What is your greatest fear?

"Bees. They just, I don't know, they make me swell up. Like, I'm almost allergic to them and something so small just strikes fear into my heart – strangely enough."

4) What do you want more of in life?

"Women. Women – not enough women. I don't know I've just been in a slump the last couple of months."

5 a) What is your greatest accomplishment?

"Re-enrolling in school – deciding I want go back to school. I just kind of did nothing for two years of my life and decided that I wasn't going anywhere so I decided to go back to school. So, I'm enrolled at (college) for next year and going to do something with that."

5 b) What are you most ashamed of?

"Not working hard enough in high school. Like, really and truly if I go back and do it again. I had lots of fun smoking weed every day with my friends and stuff but it's just not worth it in the long run. I could be two years into my education and be that much farther up on just being happy, having everything I need. But, I just 'dicked' around so here I am."

6) What makes you sad?

"That's a tough question. I'm a really happy person. (It makes me sad) when my dog is sick. You can tell when she's not happy, like when she's moping around."

7) What is the hardest thing you have ever experienced?

"When my Grandpa died in grade seven. He was a really good man. He taught me a lot of things. Just having to realize that he was in a better place and that I had to let go and he wasn't going to be there anymore. I used to spend my summers with, up with my Grandma and my Grandpa – going fishing and stuff all the time and all kinds of fun stuff. And, just not having him there any more when I go up there is definitely the hardest part."

8) What is great about you?

"I'm just a happy go lucky guy. I'm a free spirit. I don't let things get me down. I'm always in a good mood and just having a good time all the time, I guess."

9) Who are you?

"I am Billy. I like to drink beers with my friends, like to walk my dog, go long boarding, ride bikes and just, you know, have a good time I guess."

10) What question do you want me to ask you now?

"What's my biggest regret again, because I thought of a bigger regret…"

What's your biggest regret?

"I got a DUI a couple of, well a year and a half ago now. And it was a really, really bad night. One of my co-workers (at the time) rolled over his car and he killed his wife the same night because we were all just getting drunk together. So, my biggest regret is definitely putting other lives in danger while I was intoxicated."

Stranger 26 had spent a few years where he felt he "dicked" around and now it was time for change. He had made a decision to change his circumstances and enrolled in college in pursuit of something different, something better.

Growing up, I often played video games until the late hours of the evening. When I'd slip up, make a mistake, or progress slower than I'd like, I could hit the reset button and re-enter the virtual world with a fresh start. Each new life was a fresh start, a clean slate and the opportunity to learn from the mistakes I had made. Hitting the reset button on my Sega Genesis became a patterned reaction to my frustration over the gaming struggles – a parachute that helped me escape to make sure I would never lose.

Unfortunately, I can't go back to high school and re-write my tests, play better football, or spend less time partying. Oh, but if I could I would have had such an amazingly productive life. Oh to the life that could have been...

How often do you get stuck in the mental movie: "if only I knew then what I know now"? We imagine the life we could have had or the fortune we could be sitting on right now if we had just done things differently. "I wish I could start over," is something that has chimed inside the minds of many.

In the world of sports there is a concept called WIN – What's Important Now? John Wooden, legendary UCLA Basketball coach, used it to inspire his teams to unprecedented success. Forget about the last bad pass, good pass, slam dunk, or slip up – what matters is what is happening in this moment. Don't worry about what might happen – focus on the creation of each moment and what you can control. Winning in sport and life is about being present with *What's Important Now.*

What if our past wounds didn't stop us from pursuing love, pursuing dreams, pursuing truth? What if our whole life was a constant answer to "What's Important Now?" Would you let the object of your affection walk away? Would you focus on being "victorious" in the frivolous arguments with your spouse? Would the future unknowns stop you from answering the cry of your heart? Would you defer your life and personal freedom until you are retired? Or, would you forget about societal norms and travel the world now? Become an artist now? Go back to school now? You can change your life now regardless of your circumstances.

It never matters what the score is at half time – you may think it does, but it doesn't. What matters is how you finish the game, recovering after each play. It doesn't matter how difficult you're relationships have been. It doesn't matter where you have been or what you have done. Where are you going and what do you need to do to get there? Change your life, reset your circumstances, and create a new ending, beginning now.

STRANGER 27

"I do not believe in failure. It is not failure if you enjoyed the process."
- Oprah Winfrey

She and her husband joyfully farmed the fields around their African home. Events took a turn and she was forced back to Canada where she is waiting for the opportunity to return.

Breakfast stops being served at 11:00 a.m. at a local fast food establishment. My wife's voice rang inside of my head, "Remember how bad you feel when you eat fast food."

She does have a point. But, she was away for the weekend and I was craving a greasy breakfast sandwich. It was 10:47 and I walked briskly to make sure I wouldn't be refused the sausage and egg sandwich combo that my stomach craved so badly.

The fact is when my wife is gone I make poor decisions when it comes to my diet. When she's away, our kitchen becomes a ghost town. A place once bustling with activity and aromas becomes quiet, dark, and lonely. I prefer to call it *kitchen hiatus*. The funny thing is, it isn't just that I am too lazy to cook – sometimes I don't eat at all. Really, I will forget to eat when she's away. In fact, Saturday night I did not eat supper – I forgot. Eating really is more of a social thing for me. If I don't have someone to eat with, I usually default to scraping anything together in effort to tide my hunger spells.

I made it through the doors of the fast-food joint and placed my order with plenty of time to spare. After waiting only a few brief moments, there I sat, in the air-conditioned restaurant with a smile on my face. I had my greasy breakfast sandwich in hand and a newspaper in front of me.

While I sat alone enjoying my hearty breakfast, I noticed a woman beside me. She also sat alone reading the paper. We were two lonely eaters taking comfort in the refuge of a fast food breakfast. We both sat alone, only an arm's length apart. It would have been a shame if I didn't introduce myself.

Cautious at first, this para-legal assistant opened up and shared some great stories about her life. Married for 37 years, her husband works frequently over seas. Stranger 27 lived in South Africa where she owned a farm with her husband for several years and now is preparing for retirement so she can go back.

1) What is your dream job?

"That's tough because I love the job I have. But, I think my dream job would be retirement at this point. Go walk on the beach, you know, relax, read, be able to paint – all the things I don't have time for right now."

2) What fulfills you?

"Family, children, grandchildren, and painting, when I get the chance. Art – I love the creative process as much as anything. The end product isn't as important as the process. Also music – I play guitar. I enjoy creating music."

3) What is your greatest fear?

"That my husband will die before me and I'll be left alone. Just not being with him. We've been married for thirty-seven years."

4) What do you want more of in life?

"Time. Spend more time with my grandchildren, paint, play more music."

5 a) What is your greatest accomplishment?

"My children – without a doubt."

5 b) What are you most ashamed of?

"I guess that in the past I've lost my temper too often – that's probably it."

6) What makes you sad?

"Not much. I'm actually a very happy person. There's not much that makes me sad. I get upset when I see kids being abused and that kind of thing, you know, but as for in my own life: nothing."

7) What is the hardest thing you've ever experienced?

"I have a daughter who has a teenager who had many problems. I had to take her to a half-way house because she'd been told if she set another fire or pulled another knife on one of her family, or kids, or, you know, did one more thing that she's no longer be able to live at home. And the hardest thing I've ever done was drive her to that half-way house and leave her there."

8) What is great about you?

"About me? That I'm happy; that I smile. That I make other people happy. You know, I have a good sense of humor and I like to be around people and it seems that people like to be around me. So, I guess that's what's great."

9) Who are you?

"I'm a lover. I'm a mother. I'm a creative person. I love life – that probably covers it."

10) What question do you want me to ask you now?

"Where do I want to be in five years?"

Where do you want to be in five years?

"I want to be retired. I want to be on the beach in Africa. I have a place there – it's all ready. I just need to get stuff in order here and both of us to retire and then we're gone."

Why Africa?

"Because it's beautiful. We used to live there. Some of my kids were born there. Africa gets in your blood and it's difficult to leave. It's a... the people, the place, they're wonderful."

I received a look of apprehension from Stranger 27, but thankfully she was willing to let the conversation happen. What really stuck out to me in her interview was how she explained her painting and music when she said, "I love the creative process as much as anything. The end product isn't as important as the process."

The act of stepping into the fully invested action of painting your creation is magical. The brush becomes an extension of your arm, which is a conduit to a magical place – like the guitar string is the vocal cord of a soul connected to your fingertips. The essence of time is unimportant or non-existent and the hourglass is replaced by the stillness of creation. The aliveness of this moment renders the product as irrelevant.

Creation can be found in every action: doing the dishes, painting a picture, or driving a bobsleigh. It is all in your perception of the moment and your ability to create within it.

What if you considered all of your actions an expression of your creation? What is the impact it has on your life?

The product is irrelevant in the process of creation. When you are in the process of creation there is no measure. The race ends and the process continues. The canvas is covered and forever holds the precious moment of creation trapped in time. The echo of the plucked guitar is felt through the vibrations that run through your fingertips. The high jumper's victories are not enjoyed inside a trophy case but in the reminiscing of the moments of what it feels like to fly.

Find what you love and then there is no measurement. You cannot fail.

STRANGER 28

"How does one become a butterfly?" she asked. "You must want to fly
so much that you are willing to give up being a caterpillar."
- Trina Paulus

*His life was surrounded by darkness. A lonely man, he mostly resided with
corpses for much of his life. One day he looked into the empty eyes of a
lifeless young girl and decided he wanted something different. Leaving
death behind him, he chose life and instead surrounded himself by those
who could fly.*

The streets were packed with thousands of people and hundreds of booths
littered the lanes as police officers blocked off the roads for the local Sun
and Salsa Festival. I had heard about this festival for many years and had
never attended it, so it remained a mystery to me until today. A live band
played the energetic music of Eddie Herrera as people watched, snacking
away on crispy tortilla chips and salsa.

Here was the deal: it cost $3 for a bag of chips, then you walk
around the grounds to taste and judge different salsas that restaurants
carried or created for the competition. At the end of the day ballots were
collected and counted and a Sun and Salsa champion was crowned.

But salsa was not the only thing present. There were booths set up
to buy cosmetics or sunglasses, people dressed up as Star Wars characters
to promote the Star Wars club. Others promoted the Tai Chi Society, dance
studios, everything. And, of course, there was the Miss Sun and Salsa
contest.

There was action happening everywhere as we navigated through
the crowds of people. We made our way down to the last salsa stand, but
our pathway was blocked by a man standing in front of us, smiling brightly
as two parrots perched on his shoulders. His big smile matched by his wide
eyes and animated expressions. He was probably in his late forties and had
short dark hair. A large white bird with a yellow feather on top of its head
sat on his right shoulder; a smaller grey bird with orange tips on its wings

sat on his left. Before I said anything, he was taking the white one off and putting it on my arm. As he was doing it I said, "Uh… I'm not so sure about this."

I don't like birds. It's not the birds themselves, in fact, it's nothing personal against birds – it's more their large, sharp talons and their leathery feet that creep me out. Nonetheless, the bird grasped my arm and there I stood at the center flow among a sea of people, holding a parrot on my arm. Standing frozen, I held the parrot while I listened to him explain how he lived on the 27th floor of a condo tower with 6 parrots in his house and how a parrot was cheaper than a cat or dog if you amortized it over 50 years. I grabbed my recorder.

1) What is your dream job?

"I have it now. I changed my career seventeen years ago to business for myself (in) pharmaceutical and veterinary supplies so I can take a parrot to work. I love it. I was a funeral director before. Out of high school I went to mortuary college, spent twenty years in the funeral industry, and hardly saw the light of day."

2) What fulfills you?

"Mostly what fulfills me is the rewarding time that I have in training my parrots and sharing what I have with others. I don't want a nasty parrot – I want to be able to hand my parrot off to someone in public whereby they can appreciate what I've put in for work. OK, for example this (points to parrot) is seven thousand four hundred hours of training time on her alone. That is an awful lot. I keep a journal every year on every bird – it is an annual thing I do. Not only for vocabulary, but for handling and training purposes. The thing is I build up the hours and I see the appreciation that I've done by looking back when she was five years old. I thought she was great then – look at her now at twelve. She's wonderful. What's she going to be like when she's twenty? Probably better than this and that's hard to believe."

3) What is your greatest fear?

"I don't know, just maybe my greatest fear might be heights – the instability of being high up and not having the balance and tumbling down."

4) What do you want more of in life?

"Well I don't know. That's really a good question because I'm very much satisfied right now with what I'm doing. And, I just thoroughly enjoy working with these guys. This is my life. My life is parrots. And anybody that comes over to my place says, 'this must be an awful lot of work.' You know what, it's no work at all. It's just a lot of responsibility – that's the big thing."

5 a) What is your greatest accomplishment?

"My greatest accomplishment has got to be again with parrots. I've achieved more with parrots than anybody else that I know when it comes to training them, having them do tricks. This little girl (pointing at the parrot) here has got skateboards at home, roller blades, and a track on the table. It's just amazing what she will perform to do in order to get the attention from me. So, we have a very good relationship."

5 b) What are you most ashamed of?

"I don't know if I'm ashamed of anything. I'm really not ashamed of anything. I just like to get the most I can out of life, make the most of every day."

6) What makes you sad?

"A lot of times I'm called out, just because I'm with the local parrot club. I'm called out to investigate a home investigation or a rescue situation. And, to see how that bird's been treated is extremely sad because you know that bird has gone through years with that specific person or family and not been given the love that it requires. They can't be left in cages – they must be socialized. They are social creatures in a flogged area and this (being handled) is what makes them happy."

7) What is the hardest thing you have ever experienced?

"Oh, I suppose when I was a funeral director, maybe the death of a young child or a motor vehicle accident. But, you know, you adjust to that. Tomorrow is another day. But I thought to myself, 'why not look for a little bit more happiness in life and change your career – get into something that you really enjoy.' In other words, find something in life that you enjoy and do that for a living and find a way of getting paid for it. And yet, my work with my parrots is all volunteer."

8) What is great about you?

"Oh I think what's great about me is the fact that I love to share what I have when it comes to these animals. They aren't human beings but they're beings."

9) Who are you?

"I am the parrot guru."

Stranger 28 showed up before me with a large smile on his face, watching me as if he was expecting me. With thousands of people packed onto the crowded streets, amidst the loud music and activity, everything seemed to slow down as we stood in the middle of the road, the two of us with our avian companions.

I found out many fascinating things with Stranger 28. For example, his greatest fear is heights, yet he resides on the 27th floor of a high-rise apartment complex and he keeps company with those who spend hours floating in the sky.

What I loved was his comment about pursuing something different: "But I thought to myself, why not look for a little bit more happiness in life and change your career – get into something that you really enjoy."

After 17 years of keeping your nose to the grindstone, making a decision that will radically change your life can seem daunting. We develop habits and comforts, which create the perceived stability and safety around us, but forget that the structures we put up around us can block out the light. We stay in a life with caterpillar-like stillness – slowly inching around munching on leaves struggling to get to where we truly want to go, all the while resenting the rut we are stuck in. When we release ourselves from the self-imprisonment of stability and structure we open up the doors to possibilities and freedom.

Why live on the stability of the ground inching your way through life when you have the ability to fly? We all want it. We all have it. How do we access it?

Stranger 28 left the dark dungeon of his previous life and stepped into a life of freedom, choice, and fulfillment. His desire to fly led him through the path of transformation. We can transform. We can stop inching along the road of life and flutter our way to a scintillatingly creative life of meaning. It does not take miracles; it takes desire. It takes enough desire to change and a desire to fly – to leave the caterpillar behind you and emerge a butterfly.

STRANGER 29

**"You can remember her only that she is gone,
or you can cherish her memory and let it live on.
You can cry and close your mind,
be empty and turn your back.
Or you can do what she'd want,
smile, open your eyes, love and go on."**
- David Harkins

Her sweaty palms shake and the butterflies are overwhelming. Feeling a little bit woozy, she reaches into her bag for her medication. Reminding herself to breathe deeply, she tries to settle down. As the plane prepares to take off, she wonders if this will be the day?

With red swollen eyes, the woman next to us spoke into her phone, explaining why she wouldn't be home on time. She had missed her flight and was visibly upset. While trying not to be too nosy, I watched and listened as she hung up her phone, picked up a book, and read her novel while snacking on dinner at an airport restaurant.

Erin and I were on our way to spend the weekend celebrating a friend's wedding in Minneapolis. We had settled into a booth in an airport restaurant and I became aware of this woman immediately. She sat in the booth right behind my wife, so she was directly in my vision. Appearing to be in her early forties, she looked sad and I had an urge to approach her. Not only to interview her for 52 People, but I was just curious about her situation. I decided to wait until she left the restaurant.

While eating, we had made eye contact and shared a brief but connected smile with one another. This cemented my decision to approach her.

About half an hour passed before I saw her pack up and head out the door. I followed quickly behind her. "I'm going to interview her," I said to my wife as I sprinted away. Erin, now used to my random routine of taking off to interview someone, smiled up at me as I raced away, leaving her at the table alone.

Just outside of the restaurant I caught up with the woman as she pulled her luggage behind her. She flashed a little smile when I approached her, then kind of jumped back and smiled even bigger when she recognized me from inside the diner. I made my pitch and we sat on a bench and dove right in to the ten questions.

1) What is your dream job?

"Something having to do with wildlife and habitat protection – I do that now, but I'd like to get more involved if I could. Probably trying to raise money and awareness about the need to protect fish and wildlife in it's habitat. It's really important to me."

2) What fulfills you?

"Family – family and friends definitely. They're the best. It's the most important thing in my life and it's more important than anything material or things like that. It's just the best part of life."

3) What is your greatest fear?

"A plane crash. I've always been afraid of planes. I think I had a couple traumatic bad plane experiences when I was little. But, it's ironic because my job takes me flying a lot and, particularly, I fly around in little planes in Alaska and it's pretty hairy. So it's just ironic that I've kinda picked a job where I have to face my fear on a daily basis."

How do you do it?

"Deep breathing, visualization, and anxiety medication."

4) What do you want more of in life?

"Better health. I found out I just have this heart problem. It was just kinda bad luck. It was a viral infection. So, that really made me appreciate having really good health. It was kind of something I never really thought about before."

5a) What is your greatest accomplishment?

"Wow. I guess being able to have a profession that I really love is probably one of my best accomplishments so far."

5b) What are you most ashamed of?

"Probably that in the past I had abortions. That's something I really regret 'cause I was young and I really didn't think the full thing through, the kind of ramifications. And I just a personally think it was a really big mistake."

6) What makes you sad?

"Death of loved ones. I think that's probably the saddest thing."

7) What is the hardest thing you have ever experienced?

"Probably moving away from somewhere that was dear to me. So, I'm really lucky if that's the worst thing to experience. It was a hard choice. It's just someplace I wanted to stay and I moved to be close to my elderly parents."

8) What is great about you?

"I like to have fun – I think that's about the best thing. I try to always be nice and I like to be fun."

9) Who are you?

"If I was a cat and I had two rats, I'd give you one."

10) What question do you want me to ask you now?

"Where am I headed?"

Where are you headed?

"Anchorage, Alaska."

There was something about Stranger 29's very brief response about what makes her sad. "Death of loved ones."

When I met up with her, I had been on a mental roller coaster for the previous week. I was speaking to a dear friend about the messy place I was in and she shared some wise advice: "Be present and be grateful."

What I was expecting was comfort, compassion, and support, but instead, like a splash of cold water, I got washed with "be present and be grateful." There was a long pause before she followed with an emotional tale of a recent tragedy. Two young men decided to drive across the country to visit their parents and to celebrate a book release of a family friend. Two brilliant young minds destined to make a world impact were tragically taken from their loved ones when they were rear-ended by a semi-truck and the car quickly engulfed in flames. The parents lost their only two children. My friend, a mother herself, wept as she shared this story and the unimaginable pain of what it must feel like to lose your only two children: unfair, empty, heartbreaking.

I was struck with the reality of someday having children and the fear of being a provider, a father, a protector of my children their whole lives. To have them stripped away unmercifully seemed terrifying. It seems so unfair when loved ones are yanked from us unexpectedly with so much left for them to experience, to touch, to love. Why does this happen? Why did these parents lose their only two children? Why did my best friend get struck with cancer and die so young? Why does this happen?

We will never know – it is a depth of sadness that cannot be expressed in words. I often think the intensity of the pain we experience when loved ones pass is due to the unsaid words, unexpressed feelings, the things we avoid while they are alive. All of this grouped together is the ultimate pain of regret. We dwell on the unfulfilled potential of the relationship, the unfulfilled potential of the person, and the unfulfilled life – that's the tragedy.

Unfulfilled life makes me sad. The only way to carry on is to realize the fulfillment that was lived. Make a new story about the future that will be lived. Dwell in the life that was spent rather than that which was stolen. Don't turn your back on tomorrow because of yesterday. Open your eyes, love, be present and be grateful. Cherish your memories and let those who have passed away live on.

STRANGER 30

"We all leave footprints in the sand, the question is, will we be a big heal, or a great soul?"
- Unknown

He looks forward to the future to when he lies on his deathbed. He wonders, "Did I waste my life?"

It was like I was caught in a time warp in the Minneapolis airport. Erin and I were departing Minneapolis after spending a wonderful weekend celebrating our friends' marriage. Every corner I turned revealed two black leather chairs, one empty, the other one occupied by a man dressed in a pilot's uniform. The pilot was usually sitting with a newspaper spread wide open, casually glancing over top of the paper. We would make eye contact and they would respond with a masculine professional frown, nodding to the occasional passerby.

It was time to interview a pilot, so I approached one. He peeked over the paper as I pardoned myself for interrupting him and made my pitch. He quickly lifted the paper shielding his face and after listening to me he politely said no thank you. So, I continued on. About 30 feet further along the terminal was another set of chairs with another pilot. I was prepared to ask every one of them – I was going to get a pilot.

I approached pilot number 2 and sauntered up to make the pitch. He saw me coming and lowered his book. I stood over top him and requested his participation in my experiment. The young man wore glasses and squinted, bobbling his head while he considered it. He then bared his teeth as he slightly sucked in air, wincing as if in pain while his head tipped over. "I don't know," he said, making the same face you get when you suck on a sour lemon.

"You will be my 30th interview," I said.

He threw down his book. "You know what, why not. Why don't you pull up a chair."

Like Top Gun's main characters Maverick and Goose, we sat side by side. He a pilot and me his co-pilot. *You hook 'em – I'll clean 'em and fry 'em*, I wanted to say. I thought I better not – I don't want to scare this one away.

1) What is your dream job?

"I would probably say an astronaut. Just something about going to space would be cool."

2) What fulfills you?

"An element of adventure I guess. The best way I think I would describe it is kind of like an adrenaline kick. But, it's not like I have to hang off the side of a mountain. You know what I mean? Like, it could be simple, like seeing something beautiful, something like that. There is like a beauty sort of excitement to it."

3) What is your greatest fear?

"Spiders. I don't know, the creepy, hairy sort of thing – I can't take it. Particularly, the tarantulas."

4) What do you want more of in life?

"I would want more freedom."

What would you do with it?

"Probably nothing. (laugh). I'd probably be wasteful with it. But, you know just the simple things in life like – you know sitting on the couch watching TV, or the freedom to, you know, travel or, you know, just all the regular stuff that you could do in life."

5a) What is your greatest accomplishment?

"I think getting the pilot job is probably the biggest thing. It's kind of like hitting the lottery in a way. It's a hard job – a lot of experience goes into it and it's a hard job to get."

5b) What are you most ashamed of?

"I guess not making a bigger difference. Like, when I get to my deathbed and I look back, what difference did I really make in the world, you know? There's no plaque with my name on it. There's no building named after me. Not like those things are important, just there's no legacy there."

6) What makes you sad?

"Seeing loss – you know, that somebody were to lose a loved one or something like that. That look that's in their eye – that makes me sad."

7) What is the hardest thing you have ever experienced?

"I have had a pretty easy life I think. I guess the divorce of my parents. That's probably the closest I could come. Being caught in the middle, you know. They were obviously angry at each other and it didn't have anything to do with me, but it always spills over. Each one of them will use you a little bit too. 'Oh no your dad is really the horrible one here.' 'Oh no your mom's really the horrible one'."

8) What is great about you?

"Like one thing? I'm just a great person all around. (laugh). But, I love to laugh. You know, I'm not, like, the best comedian in the world, but as soon as I hear a joke I try and tell everybody that joke."

9) Who are you?

"That's a tough one. That's a fantastic question. I don't know if I've ever thought about it. I would say I am a … I'm a wanderer – I kinda go where the stream takes me."

10) What question do you want me to ask you now?

"How do you come up with these? That's not the question, but how did you come up with these? Ask me what is the most recent joke that I heard?"

What is the most recent joke that you've heard?

"It's kind of stupid but here it goes:

A guy is sitting in his house. There's a knock on the door – goes over, answers it and there's a snail. (The guy) says, 'What? Snail, get out of here.' He flicks it – the thing goes flying. A year later there's another knock on the door. It's the snail – he says "Hey what was that all about?"

---

30 Down 22 to go.

I left the interview with Stranger 30, passed several other leather chairs with several other pilots occupying them, and met my wife at our departure gate to fly home. The whole plane ride home, as we sat 35,000

145

feet above the ground, I thought about what Stranger 30 had to say in regards to what he was most ashamed of:

"I guess making not a bigger difference, you know. Like, when I get to my deathbed and I look back, you know, what difference did I really make in the world, you know? There's no plaque with my name on it. There's no building named after me. Not like those things are important, just there's no legacy there."

Legacy – something handed down by a predecessor. Everything we do in every moment has a ripple effect – It can be a look, an action, or a movement made by you that creates something in the world. Our mere presence creates a ripple of some sort. Some ripples are wide and powerful; some ripples are tiny and dissipate quickly. But, there always is a ripple. Many times we don't know what we did, but we did something. The way we are with people, the way we are with the world has an impact, whether it's intentional or not.

Reaching out to a stranger to acknowledge their existence or being present with the people in your life leaves a legacy. Notice people, notice your own brilliance, and take chances to let your life shine into the world. What you choose right now will not only leave tracks but follow you wherever you go and remain in some form whenever you leave. What if we could handpick our legacy? Would you create a legacy measured in plaques mounted on buildings or in the smiles on bright faces? Do you create space for others to fulfill their dreams or is your legacy one of pushing others down so you can see further yourself? Do you pave a path for others to see what you've seen so they can one day explore further, or do you selfishly hide your tracks so you can claim fame to reach new heights or discover new lands alone?

There is no question you will leave a footprint.

"Heal" to "soul", spread your toes and make a print that is intentional. Make your mark in this lifetime and choose what you will leave. Big or small, discreet or in the spotlight, deliver your gift to others. You will leave something behind you anyhow so why not choose? Leave a mark that heals and sink your soul into the earth so others can continue to build on the foundation you have created.

STRANGER 31

He didn't want to go. For years he resisted visiting his Grandfather who was in long term care due to suffering a severe stroke. After two years he didn't have to go any longer. No more struggle to resist but a new struggle of regret.

The sun was shining and it was a beautiful afternoon in the downtown core of the city. I was volunteering my time, hauling away items from what was formerly a constructed set for an outdoor theatre production of the famous Broadway musical "Rent". The stage was set up on one edge of a large square pond that was only about a foot deep but close to 50 yards wide. The pond was a peaceful refuge in the centre of the city and all kinds of people were gathered around the area, but one man in particular caught my attention.

He sat on the edge of the cement, dangling his bare feet into the pond. He held a journal which he was writing in, totally immersed and oblivious to his surroundings. Wearing dark sunglasses, he would periodically look up into the sky as if searching for inspiration from the warm rays of the sun. The ear buds connected to his iPod sent music into his body as he wrote intently from page to page.

I kept working, hauling items over to a large truck that was to take everything away, and would occasionally peek over in his direction to see if he was still there. Finally, while walking back from dropping a load off at the truck, I just walked past the piles of props, wood, and other items and headed straight over to the young man who appeared to be in his mid twenties. I leaned over and made my pitch.

He pulled out one of his ear buds, grinned, and set down his journal. He removed his sunglasses and looked up at me. His shoulders climbed up to his neck as he shrugged. "Sure. Ok," he said. I took off my shoes, sat down beside him, and stuck my feet in the water as we started to chat.

1) What is your dream job?

"I'd be working with Doctors Without Borders as a registered nurse somewhere in the world. I think I respect the fact that they are very outspoken about human rights abuses and they are willing to go to areas that, a lot, many of the majority of other aid organizations are not willing to go. So, I think that they are kind of willing to risk something for the people there and not just the politics."

2) What fulfills you?

"I think just being happy with people. Kind of doing your own thing and being sure of what you want and having a way to get there – that's, I think, everything. If you're not sure of where you're going or what you're doing or and who your with, it can cause a lot of confusion and anxiety. And, I think, definitely finding a place, like a niche, really just brings your whole life into a better place."

3) What is your greatest fear?

"I think having a meaningless life. You know, even if I don't get remembered and my name is not remembered by anybody else, just for myself. Working somewhere where I don't want to work with people I don't want to be with. You know, kind of that same, like finding that niche, not finding that that purpose in life – whatever it is for each individual. I think that is my biggest fear, just not being happy all the time."

4) What do you want more of in your life?

"Awareness from everybody. I think that it's definitely an age that's different from all the others because we, we are so connected to everything else in the world. You know, it used to be that you were pretty isolated in whatever region you were in the world, and now we are absolutely connected and I think we are just barely beginning to understand the ramifications of our actions. So, I think everybody needs to take a really, really hard look at their own life and not try to worry about how they're changing the world globally but understanding that they have consequences to their actions. And, that changing their own life will make a difference, and it could be that small action that makes a big difference. So, I think that I want to see more of that in my own life– kind of more of the same, more of what I'm doing. You know, I think that I'm happy with where I'm going and what I'm doing so and I've got that goal to work towards."

5 a) What is your greatest accomplishment?

"I'm not sure. I think making it this far (laugh) is an accomplishment enough. Staying really close with my family and some really solid friends I think is really hard. I've seen a lot of people walk away from their families and never look back. That's sad to me."

5b) What are you most ashamed of?

"I think, that I didn't take a lot of things seriously enough, especially in high school. Which is, I hate saying it but, it kind of was those years where you should have been looking forward and I didn't know what I wanted to do so I kind of coasted through high school, which wasn't too hard. Luckily, I could kind of get by and just coast – didn't have to bust my ass too hard. I just never finished things that I should have finished. So, I think that me not taking things seriously back in the day."

6) What makes you sad?

"Just people not caring. Like people being neglectful of themselves. Like, I'm not a smoker, I've never been a smoker, so maybe I don't understand what it's like. I hope you're not (points to me). But you know, people smoking, people driving huge vehicles. I know that you know it's not good for you, that driving huge SUVs or trucks wastes a lot of gas. So, I know that you know that. Why are you still doing it? It's that kind of attitude that, it just seems so flippant to me. It seems so arrogant that I just really can't stand that and that makes me sad."

7) What is the hardest thing you have ever had to experience?

"I went through a lot of guilt at my new job because when I was younger, I was about ten, and my grandfather had a stroke and was in a long term care hospital and I hated going to see him because it was a hospital and I was, like, ten and scared and it was depressing because he had lost a lot of his functions. So, I would always make excuses of why I didn't want to go to see him and he died about two years later and that was it. So, I think just dealing with that guilt and realizing that, you know, I was ten and it wasn't really my fault."

8) What is great about you?

"I think my ability to be kind of adaptive to each situation and to really, to feel things out. Because, I think that serves you and if you can just kind of roll with things and be really not to hard edged, not too hard lined about stuff, you're going to have a way better life. So, I think that's probably my best ability."

9) Who are you?

"I am exactly what I need to be right now."

10) What question do you want me to ask you now?

"Ask me what I'd change about myself"

What would you change about yourself?

"I think the way I kind of look down on people. I know I just said that I'm pretty adaptive but I think just being less expectant of people and just kind of letting things be – I would change that 'cause it leads to a lot of, you know, just your shaking your head hard and it does stress you out. So, I think I would change that."

I have stood before the mirror heartbroken. My eyes pierced the glass with an intense hatred for the person staring before me. Tears rolled down my face and it took every ounce not to shatter the brittle substance that projected my image back to me. I had cheated myself. I had cheated my values and invested time, money, and effort into an adventure that wasn't mine. My everyday outward facade would have told you otherwise. The cape and mask I put on in the mornings was one of heroism and happiness, but underneath it all I felt heartache and villainy. My body and mind were in pain because I was tirelessly investing myself into something that I knew others desperately wanted for me. I created a big story about how important it was for this person and that person. It was important to everyone but me. Despite success, I had failed. The smiling veneer I had created was burning an uncomfortable hole in my heart.

This has happened several times in my life. Doing things because it evokes great happiness from my parents, friends, and strangers has been my *modus operandi*. I took that feeling of fleeting approval as deep fulfillment and tricked myself into thinking it was sustainable.

Compromising, altruism, and putting others first have an important role in relationships and day-to-day life, but what am I selling my soul to? It is easy to rationalize. Do you find yourself trying the whole time to make sense of it all, to justify it? If your answer is yes, then you're cheating on yourself.

Do not live your life for the approval of others. Nobody can decide what is the best way to live your life but you.

Walk up to the mirror, take a deep breath, and stand only inches away – look through your own eyes and into your heart and see what that person has to say.

STRANGER 32

"While we try and teach our children all about life, our children teach us what life is all about."
- Anonymous

Her life is devoted to easing the pain of those who have no hope. Surrounded by ensuing death, she tries to bring light to the final moments of their life.

I sat in the late afternoon sun on a bench outside of my favorite ice cream shop. They have over 80 flavors behind the counters and a '50s decor. They even have a piano sitting in the middle of the line-up area, where guests can earn free ice cream by playing a 10-minute show. As talented as I am, ten minutes of "hot cross buns" would probably get me kicked out before a waffle cone was planted in my hands.

While I sat on the bench with a friend, I scanned the people walking in and out of the establishment. I thought that maybe I had made a poor decision in coming here to find a stranger. I spotted a woman standing alone with a puppy, so I approached and engaged. When I made my pitch and told her about the experiment, she was reluctant. She hummed and hawed and said she would do it. However, if there were any questions she didn't want to answer, she would like to bypass them.

How dangerous could I be?

I stood there with my recorder in one hand and a waffle cone filled with chocolate peanut butter swirl ice cream dripping down the other onto my shirt. She was polite, but I probably had a nice chocolate ring forming around my mouth. It certainly wouldn't have been the first time.

1) What is your dream job?

"I think dream jobs always change with where you are in your life – so what it is today isn't exactly what it is next week. (giggle). I'm kind of living my dream job. I quit. I was a nurse, so I quit. And I'm staying at home with my two kids loving life. And, we got a dog. And, I'm kind doing it."

2) What fulfills you?

"Feelings of success – and I don't mean monetary things like that, just being able to achieve some of the things you want to achieve. (*I think your dripping there.*) I think what you talked about, making a connection with people, brings more fulfillment than being a random person."

3) What is your greatest fear?

"The things I have nightmares about, being a parent, is losing a kid. Not myself, but probably them. I don't know there are a few fears (laugh)."

4) What do you want more of in life?

"Time."

What would you do with it?

"Everything. Imagine if your day was longer – how many things you could accomplish and still have time to read the paper and do all those things that you rarely take time for and then think 'Oh that was so great I should do that more often'? Yeah, more time."

5a) What is your greatest accomplishment?

(*Points to her children sitting on the bench, completely focused on their ice cream cones.*) "Those two. And, maybe him (*puppy*) if I'm lucky – I don't know it's kind of an experiment."

5b) What are you most ashamed of?

"There are certain moments in life where you reflect back and you think, 'oh man that was just so not me and I did it anyway,' and you have a lot of regret for those moments. But, I guess that's in the way you learn the most about yourself and things you'll never do again."

6) What makes you sad?

"I always cry at those commercials where they're asking for money to donate to the children. They always make me, that makes me really, really sad. It's such an abandonment of life, you know. People are so amazing and they're not even given a chance to be amazing. They have to work to eat and to be safe – all these things and it's just awful."

7) What is the hardest thing you have ever experienced?

"I don't know if you can rank them in the hardest thing. I don't think there is one thing that stands out more. I don't know if I can rank things in the hardest. I'm a palliative care nurse and probably some of the scenarios that I've seen, families that I've worked with. Particularly when I was uneducated and didn't have much experience, didn't know how to process emotions and work through things. And, when you're new at a job you always feel like you can't go to someone else – you feel more isolated. I think those were probably some of the hardest times I've had."

8) What is great about you?

"I'm willing to answer your questions. (laughing). I don't know. That would be a good question. What do other people answer? Well, I probably don't keep myself small would be the one. I am who I am. There are obviously things I can improve on. What's great about mommy?" (*looking down at her daughter who has snuggled up to her legs*).

The little girl shyly hides her face behind her ice cream cone and says, "hmm… I love you."

9) Who are you?

"A whole bunch of things. I defy labels (laughing), I don't know – I don't think you can, that would be way to simple and nobody's ever that simple, or if they are, they're lying. I'm not that simple – maybe that's the catch phrase for my t-shirt. 'Cause every day you're a little bit different and every experience you have changes you and nobody's static, so I don't know if you can say. I don't know. I'm not very good at that question, sorry."

I was sitting on my couch transcribing the interview. I had my noise reduction headphones on and was giggling away to myself as I listened to the interview. Erin was working in the kitchen and was smiling while she listened to me laugh. What was making me giggle so much? The sound of children's laughter.

While Stranger 32 and I were lost in the interview, there was some comedy happening around us. Stranger 32's little puppy had been stricken with a never-ending doggy sneeze attack and with each sneeze a chorus of hysterical children's laughter would erupt. This was happening around us and we were somewhat oblivious to it all at the time. I do remember the dog starting to sneeze, but I was so focused on getting the interview that I shut off my awareness to the life outside of the interview. Yet, as I sat in my house transcribing, I was kicking myself for not participating in the laugh-fest with these two little girls.

Later in the evening, as I was walking with my wife and our dog, we walked by three or four young children bouncing on a trampoline laughing wildly. "Whoa!" Giggle, giggle. "Whoa!" It was hilarious. Then, all of the sudden they went instantly quiet, until a little soft voice broke the silence and said in a soft, high-pitched voice. "Sorry." The bouncing and laughter quickly resumed. My wife and I couldn't help but laugh as we listened to this. It was a day of children's laughter and it certainly made me smile, it made me laugh, and it made me think.

It's amazing what children can teach us. I remember as I interviewed her mother, one of the little girls walked up and extended her cone to her mother's face to ensure her mom wouldn't miss out on the dazzling taste of her delicious ice cream.

What if we spent less time concerned with having to know everything, teaching our children what is right, and put more attention on learning from them? The serious focus we put into tasks that we makeup to be extremely important would shift to observing the world around us – watching the fluff from a dandelion fly in the wind, the piece of wood float with the rainwater into the gutter, dancing with our shadow, or asking *why*. We would play and laugh at ourselves and others as we bounce around in life and pause to take enjoyment in the comedy of a sneeze attack. Instead of trying to prove we are right, when we cause pain onto others we'd simply say 'I'm sorry'. Instead of beating around the bush or keeping things to ourselves, we'd be matter of fact and speak the truth of the situation – oblivious to the thought that it might make those around us uncomfortable. When asked a question we're not completely sure of, we'd answer with a cute smile, "Hmmm.. I love you."

Somewhere along the way we get a bit lost in adulthood. But, the children in the world give us a daily reminder that life is all about curiosity, play, laughing, truth, sharing, apologizing for our mistakes, and telling those around us that we love them.

STRANGER 33

"Eager souls, mystics and revolutionaries, may propose to refashion the world in accordance with their dreams; but evil remains, and so long as it lurks in the secret places of the heart, utopia is only the shadow of a dream"
- Nathaniel Hawthorne

He watched as cancer changed his body. After 18 years in an up-and-down marriage, a divorce changed his life. A quiet revolutionary, he uses his experiences to write about love.

Back at one of my favorite places on a sunny afternoon – the patio at Starbucks, I'd finished catching up with a friend when it was time to go to work and interview a stranger. There were two options. The first was a man who sat close to the wall looking out onto the street as he drank his coffee. The other was an older gentleman who worked diligently as he was hovered overtop his notebook periodically breaching, as if he was coming up for a sip of air, before submerging back into his work. I don't really like to disturb people while they are working, so I approached the first man. His eyes grew bigger behind his large round glasses as I approached. I made my pitch and with a soft voice he shyly said, "No thank you." I didn't want to, but my other choice was to disturb the man absorbed in his work.

He leaned on the table. His fancy white shirt was clean and unbuttoned at the top, exposing a bit of grey hair. A charismatic essence, he had a thin grey mustache and a tight line of hair running vertically down the center of his chin.

I walked up to him and bent down so he could easily see my face. As I made my pitch, I was met by the warmth of his eyes. He nodded his head as I explained 52 People and he laughed, "I'm working on a book about relationships."

1) What is your dream job?

"Writer. It allows me to explore relationships, primarily relationships that I've been involved in – in the past, in the present. Really what writing does for me: it's a discovery. I find out who I am through my writing. And primarily too, I'm writing about other people and as I write about other people my initial encounter with them or my second and third encounter is always different than the fifth, sixth and seventh encounter. And so I see something in them that I never saw upon first glance and then in turn I find out something about myself. Number one: that I should look at things more than once or twice and then it gives me something to bounce off my personality. Really, writing helps answer the question 'who am I?'"

2) What fulfills you?

"Love fulfills me. Being with a women that I dig, that also digs me, that you can be honest with – there's no curtain to be pulled over, kind of thing. So, I guess exposure. Exposure, that's what it is – revealing myself and others revealing themselves to me. Again it's the relationship."

3) What is your greatest fear?

"Not being loved. What scares me about it, I guess, is the emptiness that comes with it. Or, it's probably not believing that (I'm loved). Probably that's the greatest fear is not being loved. And the scary thing about that is that most people are loved but we have a tendency not to reveal that to the people we do love. Or, we sometimes have a misconception what love is. What is love? Those moments where I feel not loved, and usually, it's self-inflicted. So, actually I guess the scariest thing would be myself."

4) What do you want more of in your life?

"Love. Love, yeah, oh yeah. And, not only for myself but for others. That, I think that's the key. I can't make a social commentary on what ails society and how we don't spend enough time fostering relationships, but one thing I do know for certain is that the world would be a better place if we had more love than we have. And, a passion for that – to foster love."

5a) What is your greatest accomplishment?

"Having children – believing that I could do that and somehow keep my life sane and their life sane to this point. Taking on that responsibility, you know, and it's not over. They never really leave you. So, that is something to live for – something greater than yourself."

5b) What are you most ashamed of?

"A failed marriage. I have a fairly good relationship with my ex-wife. I don't like to call her my ex-wife. I like to call her my wife because I'm kinda from the thinking that there's a moment in my life where I was passionate about love and I was passionate with one person for eighteen years and had a pretty good run at it. But, it's not what it used to be, you know, so I feel remorseful about that."

6) What makes you sad?

"Poverty. Actually, that would be probably one of my other greatest fears. When I was a child, and I had it up until about two years ago maybe a year ago, when I would see poor people I would get kind of physically sick. There was a fear about that I couldn't look at them. I was telling a Franciscan monk about it one time and he said, 'Well you should feel sick.' He said it should bother you to the point where you feel sick – there's nothing wrong with that. He said, 'What is it that you fear the most?'

I said, 'Well looking into their eyes. I walk by them and I'll give them a coin, but I have a hard time looking at them because it doesn't make me feel good.'

So, he said, 'Look into their eyes.' He said, 'What you fear it's not really there, and you'll find out something about these people, you'll see something that you never saw before. You don't find it if you don't look for it.' And so I tried that and it's starting to change, but that's what bothers me the most. Poverty is the big one."

7) What is the hardest thing you have ever experienced?

"Cancer – cancer and divorce. In my particular case it wasn't so much the psychological impact of cancer but it's the physical impact. The body changes and my body has never been the same. It's been healthy, it's been alright, but it has never been what it was. But, that's interesting because it was the physical change with the cancer but it's the psychological change with the separation and divorce. I don't feel the failure or remorse about the cancer because I didn't have much to do with it. You now, it's a disease – it comes and there's no moral component tied to it. With the failed marriage there is a moral component to it. One asks them self, 'What could I have done to prevent this?'. I was going to say tragedy but it's not a tragedy. It's only a tragedy if I treat it as one."

8) What is great about you?

"Age doesn't bother me. It doesn't bother me. I'm a creative person. I play music. I've played all my life. I played in a band. I like all kind of stuff. I like hip hop. I like classical. I like jazz. I'm a teacher by trade and I've worked with young adults for 25 years. I like that. That's the group I wanted to work with, you know. I had plenty of opportunities to go elsewhere, do other things. So, I think that's it, I'm adaptable."

9) Who are you?

"I'm a revolutionary. That's who I see myself as. Would I kill for a cause? Yeah. Would I march for peace? I try to change the system quietly, like Louis Armstrong, the famous trumpet player. Everybody thinks he was a, you know, a 'cracker pleaser', but Spike Lee tells a story about that he used to play all these bars in Vegas, Chicago, New York, (and) he would never hang around the bars afterwards. What he would do: he would find where the Black Panthers were meeting and he would meet with them and he would give them cash for their cause. He was a quiet revolutionary, a quiet guerilla. And I'm kinda that. Authority, I'm suspect of authority immediately until I find out what the motivation or intent is, and then if it directly or daily affects me then I will undermine that. I'm the gingerbread man – You can't catch me. But, you do get caught – you do get caught eventually. But that's how I kind of see myself: as a revolutionary."

What are you fighting for?

"Oh, peace, love, and justice – that's an easy one."

I remember fighting for love. I remember figuratively killing for love. Ever since some of my first girlfriends, I have been fighting and killing for love. Even now with my wife I sometimes find myself slipping into the place of fighting.

My natural reaction to a girlfriend going out, doing something without me, or taking an interest in something other than me would be me in a big sulking attitude – my "try and convince them to only want to be with me" attitude. It was my futile attempt to fight and force love. Using copious amounts of energy, my insecurities screamed inside my head, *Don't let her go! She'll find someone better! Fight! Claw! Scratch! Just don't let her go!* This fighting is what I did. It made sense. If you want something you fight for it... right?

My amazing wife said to me one day after one of my greatest pouting displays,

"You know, when you do this I feel like I want to spend less time with you. When you love me before I leave, I can't wait to come back."

Wait a second... are you screwing with me? You mean all of this pouting and taking on the form of a child doesn't make you want to rush home and hop into bed with me?

This made me look back at all of my relationships where I had done this. The way I would fight to hold onto love ironically killed it. What I was fighting to preserve I was actually destroying. Erin is so brilliant.

I didn't have to fight for love. I had to open up and surrender to it. I spent too much time killing for a cause I thought was worth fighting for.

How do you fight for love? Surrender to it.

How do you fight for peace? Be at peace.

Ultimately the only one we are fighting is the one who inflicts the most damage upon us: ourselves. Peace, love, and justice are held hostage by the evil that lurks in the secret places of the heart. Pull open the curtain, expose the hidden chambers, and surrender. Let the light pour in and force the shadows to burn away, emancipating your deepest fears of pain and rejection.

STRANGER 34

"No mind is much employed upon the present; recollection and anticipation fill up almost all our moments."
- Samuel Johnson

For twenty years he lived in a waking coma. Refusing to acknowledge an undiagnosed mental illness, he went through life waiting for the other shoe to drop.

My wife and I flew down to San Francisco for a celebration. We began the morning of our first wedding anniversary by heading to place called Cafe Gratitude. Situated just outside of downtown San Francisco, it was a place we had heard about from friends and we were eager to explore its charming milieu. We ordered a vegan, live breakfast that consisted of 100 per cent whole organic foods. The names of our meals were *I am thriving, I am abundant, I am fulfilled and I am peachy*. Cafe Gratitude is as its name implies. The restaurant's philosophy is about giving thanks and being grateful and present. What a great way to celebrate the first anniversary of our marriage – to be grateful for the abundance of love we have to give each other.

We sat at a large table that could hold ten. We perched at one end, while two women sat beside us and another man and women ate at the other end. As we enjoyed our breakfast, people came to the man at the other end of the table and requested to have their picture taken with him. Everyone kept calling him Jason. I was curious and had thought about approaching him to interview him, but wasn't feeling the urge to connect. Plus, it wasn't really a situation conducive to a good interview with all the people around. I later found out he was a musician named Jason Mraz. I love his music, and it would have been neat to interview him. Oh well, not meant to be. We paid our bill and off to The Castro we went.

We arrived in The Castro District, the former home of one of the most influential gay rights activists, the late Harvey Milk. My wife went shopping inside one of the shops while I stood outside and milled about the store front, casually peeking inside the adjacent store called 'Hand Job Hair and Nails'.

A tall man with grey hair and trendy framed glasses walked out of the store my wife was in. He wore a black sweater on his thin frame and greeted me with his bright eyes. I interrupted his path with my introduction.

A native of New Zealand, Stranger 34 stopped in San Francisco on his way to a business meeting in St. Louis and met me.

1) What is your dream job?

"You say no limitations? My dream is, kind of, it's tempered by what's realistically achievable. If I was going to say time and training, all that, doesn't matter, then probably interior design or architecture. That would be, you know if you had it again. Or, a combination of design and making furniture. That would be my dream, or fantasy."

2) What fulfills you?

"Being present. Learning to be in the present – in the moment. It's a new experience for me, you know, in the context of the journey. So, learning that is kind of what I'm learning in my journey now."

3) What is your greatest fear?

"Oh, abandonment. Well, from what I understand, it links to childhood trauma. That's another part of my new discovery. I'm just getting up to a year of working with a therapist twice a week and it's kind of where we're kind of up to in the discovery – that there was significant trauma for me."

4) What do you want more of in your life?

"Touch. As a single gay man I find that's the thing that is most difficult to get. That would be it. This is my first visit to San Francisco and I had a tour guide yesterday to show me around the city and, and from time to time he would just go (motions to touch my shoulder) "Oh look at this." Only as a friendship thing, you know. And I was conscious all day at how unfamiliar that was but how nice it was. Even leaving out sex or erotic connection, just the physicality of someone was very warming, and a reminder of what I grieve the most of not having."

5a) What is your greatest accomplishment?

"Wow, wow, can you have more than one? At the moment the greatest accomplishment is, for me, is being alive. I'm really, really grateful that things a couple of years ago just nearly took me out and that life, the universe, whatever you call it, didn't let that happen. I have two adult children that I love very much and that's wonderful to be in relationship with them. So, I guess I'm acknowledging my part, the accomplishment, my part in having that relationship with them – and my part in being alive and well-ish."

5b) What are you most ashamed of?

"I'm not sure if I'm ashamed anymore, but I definitely have regret, that I had an undiagnosed mental illness for such a long time and didn't make enough effort to get the right help. So, there is a sense of lost time. Twenty years, well more than twenty – it's been there since early childhood. But, I actively started seeking help when I was thirty. Rather than blame other people for not picking up on it, you know, I didn't kind of push hard enough to get answers and get help. In that process, I lost three relationships which I attribute primarily to the fact that I hadn't figured out I was gay, other than my children's mom. But two partners I've had since then, that sorrow and loss during those years, I attribute to a result of not knowing that there was something going on – that was like this undercurrent of sabotage going on all the time. It's how it was, but it has the regret of grief and loss."

6) What makes you sad?

"Anything that pulls into loss – loss more at an existential or emotional level. People who have lost hope, lost love. Yeah, the loss of hope and love. Loss of the will to go on. It's kind of got the mirror thing that reminds me of my own loss, but feeling it for other people."

7) What is the hardest thing you have ever experienced?

"I guess it has the flip because the hardest thing has become the most wonderful thing. So, what was the hardest has kind of, with time and with insight, has become a transforming point. So, that is beginning of last year, I can tell you the day – the 4th of January of 2008, my insides, everything stopped. It just came apart. I was living by myself in western

Australia with no friends or family. My partner had suddenly ended our relationship and went out of the state. Things at work weren't going too well and I remember the afternoon well. I had a sleep for about an hour and got up, went to get out of bed and when I did my legs just gave away underneath and it was like I split into two halves. For the whole weekend I just (lay) there. I managed to pull into the bathroom and just lay on the floor shaking and staring at the wall until I got some medical help. And, then for the first six weeks I just lay and curled up thinking that it's all over. So, learning to talk again, walk again. It wasn't a physical thing; it was a mental thing. I can remember vividly, about the four week mark, the one time when I had finally made it out to the letter box and thought, 'Ok, I'm going to be Ok.' That was the hardest experience because I thought it was all over, I wasn't going to recover, and would be in an institution. That has been the most difficult thing on a personal level."

8)What is great about you?

"I think I have a funny sense of humor. And, my gentleness."

9) Who are you?

"At one level I'm a 53-year-old out gay man with a spirituality which is a kind of a mix of Christian mysticism and Buddhism – at one level. At another level I'm a year into discovering that I have DID, dissociative identity disorder, as a result of early childhood trauma. And that, through the therapy work that I've done, I've discovered that I have nine alter personalities that I'm learning to integrate in a journey of wellness. The who I am at the moment, I'll use a metaphor that has come up for me through the therapy, is the... two groups of three personalities. So, three that have a base in anxiety and three that have a base in sadness have kind of given way to what I'm beginning to learn is that authentic part of me. His name is Thomas and we have landed on an island and the island for me is the place that opens up. And, this comes back to where we started, about being present. So, the anxiety part is all about the future; the sadness part is all about the past. There is an interface, a point between the past and the future, like an infinitely thin space called the present. And if we learn or allow that space to open, it becomes the present and that's where my island is and it's the island where I land, grounded in the present and start to experience the authentic me."

My wife and I ate brunch at Cafe Gratitude and while we ate we played the Cafe Gratitude board game. I pulled a card that had the quote by Samuel Johnson written on it, and I mentioned to my wife how true this quote was for me. No more than an hour later I was interviewing Stranger 34 who spoke about his journey in the discovery of presence.

Stranger 34 spoke about the anxiety that comes with the future, the sadness that comes with the past, and the infinitely thin space in between which is the present.

When I look at how I operate on a daily basis, the majority of my idle time is spent anticipating the future – the mental 'what-iff' movies that create horrible possibilities or fantasy like dreams. If it isn't the anticipation of the future, the idle time is spent in the past, focused on regrets, visualizing 'do-over's', or basking in past accolades.

Oh how elusive that infinitely thin space is. It takes work to be present. It takes work to clear all the clutter that the mind likes to fill the empty space with, but when we do it allows for tremendous growth and authenticity.

The present smacks us in the face in those precious moments when nature has seized everything else and there is nothing but the crisp air or the vast beauty around us. True connection, when you are deeply connected to the person you are with, and true intimacy can keep us in the present, whether you are making love or simply invested in the person or people you are with. Not worrying about your image, your day, or tomorrow, nothing but the power of connection and free flowing conversation can create a connection to the present. Everyone has experienced this in some way. Like Eleanor Roosevelt said: "Yesterday is history, tomorrow is a mystery, but today is a gift... and that is why they call it the present."

Everybody enjoys receiving gifts and the best gift you can give yourself and others is your love of the present. Let recollection stay behind you and stop mobilizing forces for future unknown battles. Relax, breath, and be grateful for what you can give: Presence.

STRANGER 35

"You were born with potential
You were born with ideals and dreams
You were born with greatness
You were born with wings
You are not meant for crawling, so don't.
You have wings
Learn to use them, and fly."
- Rumi

Imagine doing what you feel you were born to do – waking up every day
knowing you were fulfilling your mission. As the turbines fire and he
checks his gauges, he knows, without a doubt, that he was born to spend
his time amongst the clouds.

After celebrating my first wedding anniversary with my beautiful wife, she
flew home and I traveled north of San Francisco to engage in another
week-long Co-active™ leadership retreat with little-to-no communication
with the outside world. At the completion of the week I was anxious to
find out what was happening to my favorite college football team. I arrived
at the airport just over an hour before my flight was scheduled to depart for
home. I missed the entire first half of the football game and scrambled to
an airport bar to watch as much as I could before my departure.

After the bartender kindly tracked the game down for me on the
television, I scarfed down a panini sandwich and a cranberry juice. I
watched the University of Colorado take the opening drive of the second
half down the field for a score. On a commercial break I ran to my gate and
had my boarding pass pre-checked and quickly returned to the game. I was
standing behind my former chair at the bar and standing behind me was a
man looking over my shoulder. I apologized for blocking his way and
asked him if he'd like to sit down. He kindly declined and said he would
just stand and drink his beer. He was slightly taller than me and was about
40-years-old and wore a lightly colored shirt with a brown and yellow

flowery pattern on it. His greying hair was slicked back and he had a strong-jawed smile and a confident look to him.

I had the feeling I was going to interview him so I took the recorder out of my pocket and held it in my hand. A conversation took place inside my head about whether or not I was going to ask him or get someone else – maybe someone on the plane to be Stranger 35. As this conversation was taking place, a voice spoke to me from behind.

"What is that?" The man said, pointing towards my hand.

"Oh, it's a voice recorder."

He smiled and nodded. "I thought it was a phone and was going to ask you where you got a phone that small."

"No, but actually I was going to ask you if I could interview you."

Stranger 35 was a military pilot who was on his way to compete in a large competition of high speed airplane races in Reno, Nevada.

1) What is your dream job?

"I'm doing it. It's what I came out of the womb wanting to do, So that's what I do, so...."

2) What fulfills you?

"Family. The love of the family. The love and support that I get from my family."

3) What is your greatest fear?

"Death because I think it will be painful."

4) What do you want more out of life?

"End play. I want to know what I'm working for is worth it. Just, what are you working for.?

What are you working for?

"The end play."

5a) What is your greatest accomplishment?

"The silver wings I wear on my chest – it's what I was born to do."

5b) What are you most ashamed of?

"Alcoholic transgressions.

Do you want to elaborate?

"No, because they are just summarized in one big lump."

6) What makes you sad?

"Separation from the people I love."

7) What is the hardest thing you have ever experienced?

"Death. You know, death of loved ones or other pilots. Seeing the death when it happens."

8) What is great about you?

"I'm well travelled."

9) Who are you?

"A pilot. I love to fly."

10) What question do you want to ask me now?

"Can I buy you a beer?"

Can I buy you a beer?

"Do we have time?"

This was a short and sweet interview – probably due to the fact that both of us were minutes away from our separate departures. Stranger 35 was hesitant to do the interview and asked if he could decline questions if they were too intrusive. He wasn't much for elaborating or diving deep into his answers and resisted exploring them further than his brief points.

What I loved was the straight up comment that he was born to fly and that's what he loves doing. But, more questions emerged with this answer. What is it about flying that makes you so fulfilled? If you were born to fly, what happens when you stop stepping into the cockpit? Does your purpose on this planet cease to exist? What is it to fully express your life purpose? Life purpose is wonderful exploration that can open new doors and help you see your life in a completely new way. It is also something that you continue to craft and re-craft as you find out more about yourself.

What do I know about my life purpose right now? My life purpose is to shine inspiration on others so they can see their own greatness. This is what I know about myself right now and this will certainly shift and be re-sculpted many times as my life continues and learning goes on. Understanding my purpose gives me the ability to connect with what I'm doing in a more meaningful way.

Had you asked me 4 or 5 years ago what my purpose was in life I would have told you that it was to drive my bobsleigh as fast as I could and inspire people along the way. I knew I wanted to inspire others to do something. What I eventually realized was that driving a bobsleigh was not the only way to do it. Speaking, coaching, writing, and simple day-to-day connection has helped me inspire others and be inspired through others.

My purpose is to help others realize they have wings and that they can use them to fly. As I see them take off and soar, I become inspired at the phenomenon of flight and the ability we all have to fly. Seeing this in others allows me to take flight. When we get chills from watching professional athletes overcome great obstacles and achieve greatness or watch an unsuspecting person do something remarkable, we become inspired. The inspiration lies in the inner wisdom that knows we have this same ability. It may not be displayed in the same way as a Super Bowl winning touchdown pass or a passionate song, but we all have wings.

Do not allow yourself to crawl. You were born to fly in your own great way. Find your wings and soar.

STRANGER 36

"A baby is born with a need to be loved – and never outgrows it."
- Frank A. Clark

A million thoughts race through her head as she waits alone in the bathroom. "Still a few more seconds... What will I do? How will we do it?" Her stomach drops as she experiences a moment of fear – She's pregnant.

It was a sleepless night on Saturday. I was like a kid on Christmas Eve, tossing and turning, waiting for the sun to rise and finally bring with it the opening kickoffs of the first NFL Sunday. NFL Sundays are a big event each week for me. Family and friends gather over at my brother's place for a full day of football, snacking, and more snacking.

I left my house at 8:30 a.m. and walked with my dog to meet my brother and his family to begin the traditional coffee walk. We start our Sundays by grabbing a coffee at the neighborhood Cafe. Unfortunately for us, the espresso machine was broken so I had to deviate from ordering my staple – a large 'with room' Americano – and was forced to purchase a boring medium roast blend. While my brother and I waited for our coffees I took a quick scan of the place to see if there were any potential Strangers sitting at any of the tables.

There was a young woman with long dark hair sitting alone at a table with newspaper spread across it drinking her coffee. I watched to see if there was anyone coming to join her and it seemed like every time I glanced over to her she would bust me looking at her. She was the one.

I asked my brother to take my dog with him back to the house as I was going to attempt to interview her. He loaded up the drinks and took off while I walked over to the table, introduced myself, and made my pitch.

1) What is your dream job?

"I would create a construction training program for immigrant women to integrate them into the society and fill the labour shortage in the city appropriately. Because, I've taught English as a second language for the immigration and refugee programs and I don't see the academic route as the only way. So, there are some construction schools here, and I teach at them, but they're not suited to meet the market."

2) What fulfills you?

"Simply smiling faces on those passing me bye. And, knowing that they are full of love and joy and a smile can share that with somebody else. If I have it somebody else can too."

3) What is your greatest fear?

"I'm pregnant right now and bringing a life into this world is my greatest fear because it was unexpected and it has changed my entire life course at this point. It's joyous. However, it is a greatest fear."

4) What do you want more of in your life?

"I want more money. I want to earn more money by helping other people though not just by having more money. I would be able to build better social programs here and abroad and integrate education and construction skills which I really think literally build somebody's future."

5a) What is your greatest accomplishment?

"Having traveled to India by myself at 17 for the first time and volunteering in an orphanage and toughing it out. And, understanding what it is in society to be a minority and to be 'less than' even in a place where everything is deemed in the paper that they're 'less than.' But, when you put yourself in the middle of somewhere and you're the only one, you really start to understand what it's like to be alone."

5b) What are you most ashamed of?

"Having had a serious drug and alcohol addiction. I got sober three and a half years ago, but there are parts of my past that creep into my life at all times and they can come up. I avoid Facebook because of it. I just don't want any unrealistic connections with things from my past that I don't have to go back to. I accept it, but I don't want to go back there."

6) What makes you sad?

"Loneliness. Somebody else not having somebody to hug. Not understanding love. Not understanding what it means to share something – what it means to receive without necessity."

7) What is the hardest thing you have ever experienced?

"I moved to Korea to get sober and taught English for a year in a college after I graduated from university and found a program there. But, at the same time I was a victim of a sexual assault by a member of the American military. There's about a hundred thousand troops in the middle of Seoul and a lot of them live outside. There's a possibility I was drugged or something at that time. And, that was one of the hardest things I've ever had to overcome and experience and be all alone over there to come out of. But, you can move on."

8) What is great about you?

"That I love my life. I love my life and I share that all over. I don't just have one job – I have lots of things on the go. And, just to bring joy. I mean I've been down, I'm still around people who are down, and it helps to encourage them to pick it back up."

9) Who are you?

"I'm a beautiful woman who is going to go a long way in this world and takes every experience as something that happens as every bit of my day. And I'm love. I'm love."

The timing of the strangers that arrive in my life is impeccable. About 13 weeks prior to meeting Stranger 36, my face turned blank, my mouth stuck open as a million thoughts raced through my head. Despite the chaos, there was silence and momentary paralysis. My wife stood in front of me with tears of joy in her eyes waiting for me to say something.

"Wow."

That's what came out of my mouth after my wife told me we were pregnant.

Wow?

No tears of joy, no jumping up and down, nothing but paralysis. I could not comprehend the words she was saying. What I was saying inside my head was, *But what about our plans to travel across North America inspiring people to live the lives they want! What about all of these dreams and ideas we have?* The next sentence was the very scary thought: *But I forget to feed myself some days, how can I be responsible for another being?*

None of this was the reaction my wife was expecting, nor hoping for. We had spoken about trying to get pregnant and this was something that we both felt we were ready for. After years of "practicing", we had stepped up the game to "trying". Well, when we didn't get pregnant the first time around I started planning the next phase of our life: 8 to 12 months traveling by trailer across North America conducting a new social experiment and changing the lives of individuals, communities, and the world.

As soon as these plans started, they were forced to an abrupt halt. *Breathe.* I found out I was going to be a father. On, or around, March 20th I would be the father of a little baby, or two, or six, however many were growing inside of Erin. And, I was excited. I was excited to receive my greatest teacher – the one who would undoubtedly test me and teach me and love me. I was excited to have another hand to hold, feel another heart beat close to mine, to sit back and dream big dreams with. I was excited for the challenges that lay ahead for Erin and I – for our relationship, for us as individuals, and for the lifestyle that we were committed to living.

I was also terrified. I was terrified of the responsibility. I was terrified at the possibility something was to go wrong with the pregnancy. I was terrified that my wife and I would slide into a convenient lifestyle that pushed our dreams aside and pushed us apart. All of these things ran through my head at times when I dreamt about how this new life was going to look come March 20th.

Thanks to Stranger 36 I know I'll be OK – just like I know she'll be OK. During our interview she reminded me who we all are and what never-ending resource I can always provide my new child with: love. When we are grounded, inspired, and connected, that is who we are. That is who I am and that is what I know I can give my wife and child.

There may be times when we cannot give our children some of the things that they want, but we always have the ability to give them all the love they need. That makes me feel better.

STRANGER 37

"What I do you cannot do; but what you do, I cannot do. The needs are great, and none of us, including me, ever do great things. But we can all do small things, with great love, and together we can do something wonderful."
- Mother Teresa

He watched proudly as his son began to talk, walk, and eventually run. The years seemed to fly by as he was soon in school and going through the struggles that kids go through. Helping him as best he could along the way, never in his worst nightmares had he thought his son would take his own life.

Unusual autumn rain fell from the sky and soaked my sweater as I worked feverishly to empty my plastics, paper, and cardboard into the big green recycling bin near the grocery store. I had slept in and already had broken the normal morning ritual to begin NFL Sundays.

Originally, I was hoping to interview someone else unloading recycling. But, at a place that was usually quite busy, I was the only one recycling during a chilly Sunday rainfall. Once the last load of paper was shoved into the bin I figured I'd fill up my car and check out a possible stranger at the gas station.

A woman filled up her car in front of me and I quickly targeted her for the interview, but she paid and took off before I could approach her. A few contingency plans ran through my head. I was the only car left and I went inside to pay for my fuel. There were two men at the counter. It crossed my mind to ask one of them, but not enough to seriously consider it so I went back outside to my car. Another car pulled up beside me just as I walked out, and a man got out and stood next to the pump. He stood about five-foot-ten and wore a blue long-sleeve shirt. The top of his head was bald, but the sides hosted thick brown hair, the same color as the mustache and goatee that grew in an intimidating fashion on his face. I had an urge to approach him, but I got inside my vehicle and thought about another plan. As I sat there for only a few moments, the urge overcame me and I hopped back out of the car and walked up to the man. Slightly intimidated, I approached him and made my pitch. He responded unenthusiastically, but he was willing to participate as he filled his car at the gas pump.

1) What is your dream job?

"Boy that's a tough one. Probably overseeing something like the Franklin Dream Association – that's Billy Graham's one. So, ministry stuff."

2) What fulfills you?

"Spending time with God."

What is it about that that fulfills you?

"That's a pretty deep question right now because two months ago I lost my son. He committed suicide. So, praying to God is the thing that gives me peace. It fills me up and comforts me. And, with spending that time with Him I know I don't have to worry about taking care of everything because He is watching over everything that I do and He'll guide the steps that I take."

3) What is your greatest fear?

"That people will figure out that I'm not capable of doing something – just that I won't live up to the expectations of others."

4) What do you want more of in your life?

"More personal relationships with others."

5a) What is your greatest accomplishment?

"The friends that I have during this time – those friends who have surrounded me and supported me and taken care of and gotten me through all kinds of problems. And, with them I'm able to do things I wouldn't be able to do on my own. I don't have to carry the world by myself. I have a whole bunch of people helping me with that."

5b) What are you most ashamed of?

"Probably how I've not made those relationships a priority: relationships with my kids and the relationships with others around me. And, waiting for them to come to me and not me going to them."

6) What makes you sad?

"It's a very distinct thing. It's when people are compassionate to others. It makes me sad, but it's a happy sadness. It's when they reach out and support and do things to lift somebody up."

7) What is the hardest thing you have ever experienced?

"My son committing suicide. That's pretty hard."

8) What is great about you?

"I'm very supportive – very willing to help other people out, almost to a fault. Coming along and supporting them and giving of myself without conditions."

9) Who are you?

"I'm every other guy out there, except I'm the one who's normal. But, I'm abnormal today because I'm normal. I'm looking for the people that are hurt and I'm trying to keep my own life from being a big mess. Spinning on a… racing down the road trying not to lose control as I do that."

10) What question do you want me to ask you now?

"How can we get through things when the whole world seems to be against us?"

How can you get through things when the whole world seems to be against you?

"You don't depend on your own strength. You don't do things on your own power. You set aside your pride and your need to control things and you look to God to give you the strength. And, you put your trust in Him and you set aside your fears and you trust that He's going to take care of you and that whatever He has for you to do next is the right thing for you."

I wanted to reach out and engulf Stranger 37 in a massive bear hug as he spoke about his son. I was caught off guard and left speechless. I was also enamored at the gratitude he showed for the great friends and family who have stood with him through the difficult times. This had been an invaluable gift during the last few months in his life.

I've spent many years of my life thinking that I could shoulder the weight of all of the heavy problems thrown to me by the universe – sometimes pushing with all my might against the forces against me or holding on to the dizzying merry-go-round of life as it picks up in speed and my grip becomes hardened steel as I refuse to let go and fearfully hold on. I have pushed alone, have held on alone, and – as a result – have spent some years of my life lonely and exhausted.

Every human brings their gifts with them as they journey through their life. They meet others and support one another to create something greater. A support system that functions as a unified group exceeds the sum of it's individual parts. This powerful sum provides both solace during tragedy and sweetens the celebrations of victory. When we lean on others and others lean on us we get to experience the magic of collaboration, the alchemy of connection, the power of trust, and the phenomenon of 1+1=3.

Stop holding the weight of your life all alone. Ask for help. Ask for someone to grab a corner and lighten your load or to catch you if you let go. We need others to lean into us as much as we need to lean into others. This reciprocity is what inspires us to live great lives, achieve great dreams, and experience the wonder of life. We are in this thing together.

STRANGER 38

"Given the choice between the experience of pain and nothing, I would choose pain"
- William Faulkner

Diagnosed with cancer, he was written off by others. It took him weeks for the reality to settle in that he had the big "C". Facing the most challenging experience of his life, he now credits it to living a more fulfilling existence.

Saturday was a busy day. Erin and I were still living in a mess as we had spent the week moving into our new place. Despite the boxes littered around the house, we escaped the mess and began our day by attending a friend's book signing. After visiting for a while and hanging around the book launch, we headed back to our old house to clean baseboards, fill in nail holes, vacuum, and double check that nothing was left behind. It was the last day I'd be in the townhouse that I bought over 7 years ago.

Some of the fondest memories I have of that place surround the time when I first bought it. The teal carpet and pink window coverings were torn out and for the first month I lived in a construction zone as renovations unfolded. Long days were spent with my friend Dallas, who was on long-term disability as he fought his cancer. I would tear out carpet or paint and he would help when he could or sometimes just sit and keep me company during the day. It was these precious moments that made it tough to leave the keys on the counter of my first home.

The day wasn't over. My friends and I participate in an annual event called Light the Night. Thousands of people embarked on a five-kilometer walk in honour of survivors and those inflicted to raise money for the Leukemia and Lymphoma Society.

We walked among the masses along a narrow bicycle path. About half way through our walk my attention was caught by a man who appeared to be in his late forties. He was tall and had short curly hair that was splashed with salt–and–pepper colour. He walked alone amidst the crowd, appearing deep in thought as the sea of people slowly took its course. I thought several times to approach and ask him, but I waited. Every time he would escape my sight he would reappear. Finally, I jogged up to him and made my pitch.

"As long as they aren't about finances," he said after agreeing to do the interview.

1) What is your dream job?

"Working for Habitat for Humanity – so I can give back."

2) What fulfills you?

"Being. Being rather than doing."

3) What is your greatest fear?

"I'm not sure. I used to be afraid, but I can't think of what I'm afraid of now. I guess being forgotten – not making a difference for some reason."

4) What do you want more of in life?

"I guess happiness. Satisfaction, happiness, joy, good feelings."

5a) What is your greatest accomplishment?

"The last job I held. I got pretty good at it and I was there for about 20 years and I was able to help a lot of people with the problems they were having on the job."

5b) What are you most ashamed of?

"Not waking up sooner. Living unconsciously."

6) What makes you sad?

"People who don't get it. People who are suffering. That's about it. People who are not awake yet."

7) What is the hardest thing you have ever experienced?

"On the cancer ward – being in the cancer ward. Right after I was diagnosed there was about one a week where I call it the 'deer in the headlights' faze where you don't know what to think or what to do and that was kind of a lost feeling."

8)What is great about you?

"Helpfulness. I'm not sure. Modesty. I'm friendly, I guess."

9) Who are you?

"I am being. I am here. I am present. Is that enough? I don't know, I guess I'm unique."

10) What question do you want me to ask you now?

"I don't know what would you like to ask me?"

How long have you been in remission?

"Since February."

What type of cancer?

"Non-Hodgkins Lymphoma. If I had to do it over again I would choose the cancer. I have never met a nicer bunch of people on the cancer wards – who supported me – and the medical profession and all the other supports. And I know my mind wouldn't be anywhere near where it is now if I didn't go through that and now I appreciate every moment here."

––––––––––––––––

There are times where we coast through life, unconsciously go about our routines, drive to work the whole time with our minds lost in the past or future. Like robots, we lumber through our days hoping for something better, something different, all the while missing the life that is happening around us. We can sleep walk through most of our lives and continue to sleep walk until tragedy strikes.

It often takes the death of a loved one for family and friends to get together as a tight community. It can take a terminal illness to see time as the most precious resource, not to be wasted frivolously. It can take a crippling accident to force us to swallow our pride and learn to ask for help. It can take someone to lose life before we start questioning the meaning of our own. Tragedy grabs us by the shoulders and shakes our body, the foundation that we stand on, and the cobwebs from inside our heads so we can wake up.

Experiencing this pain can be a gift. Like a muscle must tear to grow bigger and stronger, the pain in our lives can lead to tremendous personal growth – the pain that will provide greater perspective for future experiences, pain that provides the wisdom of life.

I used to think it was easier to steer clear from the pain of heartbreak than to subject myself to it. After a painful break-up, I feared stepping into another relationship that was vulnerable could result in another gut-wrenching feeling of not being accepted and loved. But what is the alternative? Living life alone?

There are many along with me who have been hurt so badly, they fear to venture back out into the internal battlefield of love. But, I did it. And, despite my fears and pains that have come along with it, my experience has been even greater because of the lessons I learned from those events. If given the choice, I choose pain. The alternative is nothing.

STRANGER 39

"Travel is more than the seeing of sights. It is a change that goes on, deep and permanent, in the ideas of living."
- Miriam Beard

A quintessential achiever, she was only 26 when she earned her PHD. Yet, despite all she has done, the only question that rings inside her head is "will I be alone forever?"

Snow arrived on Sunday and left the ground covered with a thin layer of white powder. Veteran blades of green grass poked out, confused at the unexpected early arrival. While the cold weather came, I spent the majority of my weekend indoors.

I was locked up all weekend in the basement of a rural community centre surrounded by ravens, foxes, grizzly bears, hawks, wolves, and buffalo. A traveling zoo? No. Taxidermist? Nope. The basement was also full of drums and rattles and housed a master Shaman. The workshop was a two day, 8 hour-a-day event based on the Native American art of Shamanism. The Shamanic workshop was focused on healing and energy.

There was interaction among the group throughout the weekend. Still at the end of the workshop I hadn't spoken to some of the other twenty or so participants. I had a gut feeling to interview a woman that had spent the weekend sitting about ten feet to my left. She was a petite woman with dark hair and large brown eyes. A university professor, she agreed instantly when I asked her to be Stranger 39.

1) What is your dream job?

"If I could step into my dream job tomorrow I would have two components. I would take pictures of places all over the world, places and people all over the world, that would have elements of healing, or love, or compassion in them. So, they would invoke those kinds of feelings in others who viewed them and also it would bring the world together to actually see that there is beauty everywhere. And then, I would also like to be able to continue to learn and as well teach different healing modalities."

2) What fulfills you?

"The first thing that came to mind was food. (laughing). Yummy, delicious, very flavorful food. Taking pictures. Without having time constraints or people constraints, being able to travel in the biggest sense of the word. So, being a traveler in the sense that it's being able to travel with your taste buds, travel with your eyes, travel with your feet and legs. So, seeing, tasting, and meeting people from all over the world, and tasting new things from all over the world, seeing new sights from all over the world – that's when I'm most happiest."

3) What is your greatest fear?

"Failing. Not meeting. Not doing what I was meant to be doing in this lifetime. So, missing the mark or not even seeing where the mark was. Or, being to scared to take up the staff to do what I'm supposed to do. And then, because I'm a raven, it's not so much a fear as it is a dread that I'd have to do this journey in this life alone, without a partner. I'm very comfortable doing so, but I'd really rather not."

4) What do you want more of in life?

"Travel, more travel – anywhere I haven't gone before."

5a) What is your greatest accomplishment?

"I can think of a couple in different categories. At the risk of being a nerd, my greatest academic or career accomplishment, I got a Phd at the age of twenty six. In terms of greatest accomplishment for me on a spiritual level, I learned how to do Reiki and I was able to help my Mom with her pain and suffering when she was dying from terminal cancer. And then, on an emotional level, my mom and I were able to heal anything between us before she passed away and so that was a great accomplishment. Because, even though she's gone and I miss her terribly, we were able to heal stuff before she left. So, I think that's about it. Oh, and also another great accomplishment is every day when I push myself outside my comfort zone and I do something that scares me but I know is right is a great accomplishment for me."

5b) What are you most ashamed of?

"Being petty. So, if I'm not able to be the wise 'Yoda' soul, I get my feelings hurt and I take things personally when I know it's not to do with me personally, sometimes when I'm tired and fatigued I slip back into that stage. When the question is what I'm most ashamed of again? I don't know if it's ashamed, but not being aware – being unconscious until I was in my mid-thirties. And, so I wasn't aware that I was doing things that weren't in my soul's best interest until I woke up. So, I don't know if I'm ashamed or just disappointed that I didn't wake up sooner, but at least I woke up."

6) What makes you sad?

"People hurting and not being able to see that they are able to heal themselves. So, people in hurting situations and you can see the little five year old, the little three year old, the little ten year old or the twenty year old – something that happened to them and they are stuck in that situation. And, for whatever reason they aren't able to see that there is light, that there is hope, and that they can actually – just by thinking about things differently by thinking positively – that they can step into a completely different world. If they just realized that thoughts are energy and that words have energy and if they just changed their vocabulary, changed what they thought about every day, their whole world would change so quickly. So, that is probably what does it the most for me."

7) What is the hardest thing you have ever experienced?

"Well, because I'm a raven – that's my power animal, I'm a raven – hardest thing I've had to experience is separation from spouse or separation from a serious relationships. And, that was even worse than my mom passing away. My mom passing away – we were able to heal that, spend some time. She was suffering so it was time for her to go. But, ravens need to bond, to merge, to have a soul mate for life. When I have separated from those that I thought were going to be that person in my life that was the worst part for sure."

8) What is great about you?

"That I can be, I can still be, a little kid and not have to feel I have to be an adult. So I can bring a Yoda (doll) and strap him in the front seat of the car with me when I drive through the mountains and who cares. I have a big drawer in my desk at the university that is full of snack food. The fact that, yes, I do have all seven seasons of 'Star Trek – Deep Space

Nine' and I've watched them all as well and I know every line to the first 'Star Wars' movie – the real star wars movie. So, the fact that I can be a little kid and enjoy the little kid things and get excited about a chocolate bar or get excited about the fact that I can't wait to see this movie or that kind of thing. I don't know if that you would consider that great but it's something that other people enjoy as well."

9) Who are you?

"I'll explain it in nouns. I'm Raven – that's my power animal. By profession, I am a professor. By training, I'm a psychologist. By life view, I'm a traveler. And, in terms of how I view the world and magic and the rest of it, I would say I'm a child who always seems to continue to believe in magic and wonder and middle earth and all those things. I'm also somebody who believes in the power of love and believes the power of good and kindness and the fact that words have energies, thoughts have energies. And, I'm also a lifelong learner on this journey of life. So, I want to leave this life and take the towel and wring it dry. I want to soak the most out of every single day that I can while I walk this earth. So, that would probably sum it up."

10) What question do you want me to ask you now?

"Ok, do you believe in magic?"

Do you believe in magic?

"Yes, it is everywhere. There are orbs in my living room – I can see them when I take pictures with my camera. I saw sound waves bounce off trees at the Folk Fest this year – I could see them with my own eyes. My mother sends me certain animals when she knows I need the messages. So, there is magic everywhere. You just have to look for it, and you have to believe, and when you open your eyes and you take whatever pill they say in the Matrix – I can never get it right – you take the blue or the red pill and you actually start to believe the world is so much better and so much safer and so much more magical and supportive than we ever could believe before. So, I would say yeah, I do believe in magic – absolutely."

I was among three others who stood in front of a twenty person class at a Co-active™ leadership program in Northern California about three months before meeting Stranger 39. We were in the middle of an exercise and were instructed to act out our favorite mode of transportation. I started walking as if going for a Sunday stroll, someone else pretended to drive a car in a wild chase, another rode a bicycle, and then there was the young girl in her late twenties who sat cross legged on the floor and started meditating. *Mode of transportation?*

What I love about what Stranger 39 said was, 'traveling in every sense of the word.' The way she said it created a picture inside my head that traveling is more than physically changing your location. Traveling is choosing to experience things differently. This idea made me think about the meditating traveler in Northern California and the many different forms of transporting yourself out of your ordinary reality.

I love traveling. I love it because it's like being a kid again, experiencing life for the first time – the different smells, the different tastes, sights, everything is different in big and subtle ways. When we embark on journeys around the world we generally slow down, absorb more of our surroundings, become more present, and appreciate the gifts that the world has to offer. But, we don't need to hop on a plane or endure a long road trip to experience life differently. We can experience a different world from where we are.

Slowing down the way you eat or walk allows you to experience life in a different way. Escaping the mold of normality in any way takes you out of your current structure and into foreign territory.

To travel is to be alive. To be alive is to fully experience your life through living with ever evolving eyes, ears, nose, and mind. 'Traveling in every sense of the word' is a journey towards finding your true home – a home where aliveness, inspiration, creativity and curiosity reside together.

STRANGER 40

"I would much rather have regrets about not doing what people said, than regretting not doing what my heart led me to and wondering what life had been like if I'd just been myself."
- Brittany Renée

He had wondered why his parents were no longer living together, but he gets it now. He often spends the stretches in between visiting his father wondering what it would be like to be with him all the time. After spending time trying to make other people happy, he has decided to be his own person.

It had been a crazy few months. My wife left for the weekend to visit her parents and I stayed back home in our new place to work on the house. We decided to put a yoga and meditation room in our basement, so I conscripted my father and brother to help me lay down the floor. After working away all weekend long, the room was basically done, but the list of other "To Do" tasks had actually grown: hedges, more painting, more unpacking, garage needed organizing. And, oh yeah, I also had to work so we could pay for the house we moved into.

As the days went by I became more excited about the arrival of our first child. The switching back and forth between fear and excitement was starting to suspend more on the excitement side. Erin's gorgeous little belly was quickly expanding and we were close to seeing that little thing during our first ultrasound. It was hard to imagine that by March I would be holding our baby. How would we raise our child? What world would our child grow up in? What would a young child think about life and the world we live in?

On a crisp Sunday morning while walking my dog, I walked past a young boy who stood beside his bike. A blond haired, blue eyed boy of nine years stopped what he was doing and shared his wisdom with me.

1) What is your dream job?

"That one's hard. I would love to be a person who goes out and does his own thing. He just goes out. Like, if he has a dirt bike he goes dirt biking with a friend – just takes a friend with him. Go quading – fun stuff like that."

2) What fulfills you?

"Well, one thing that I love that makes me feel like that is snowboarding. It's just getting out on the hill just doing what you feel like. It's just the freedom that you get. It's talking to friends and it's awesome."

3) What is your greatest fear?

"Well, sometimes if my friends are in trouble. Like with family and stuff, and if one of them has a 'heart attack' I really try and help them. But, if it keeps going – I hate to let it go on I guess."

4) What do you want more of in life?

"More time to spend with my Dad."

5a) What is your greatest accomplishment?

"Probably my greatest accomplishment would be one time when I was wakeboarding, –well not wakeboarding, I was skiing – I just felt like trying skiing on one ski so I went on the wake and I just dropped it and I was up. I just stayed up and now I can do it."

5b) What are you most ashamed of?

"Well, one thing is that sometimes if people don't listen to me I get frustrated and I really don't like getting frustrated."

6) What makes you sad?

"When someone dies. When my brother gets hurt, well if he gets like really badly hurt. Sometimes when I get hurt I cry."

7) What is the hardest thing you have ever experienced?

"Well, I used to try and be like somebody else, like Tony Hawk or somebody, because I just thought he was so cool. But now I'm just myself. I be myself. I do what I want to do. I don't do what he likes to do – I don't want to. I'm just myself now."

8) What is great about you?

"A lot of people like to say that I'm polite – nice – and that's pretty much it."

9) Who are you?

"I am a person that likes doing his own thing. I like helping people. I like doing stuff with other people to take up my time."

10) What question do you want me to ask you now?

"Maybe, what is your favorite thing to do in your life?"

What is your favorite thing to do in life?

"Well, I just got introduced to golfing and I really enjoy that. We went out to the driving range yesterday. I think I'll enjoy golf. And, I love snowboarding. I love riding my dirt bike. I love quading with friends."

The cool blue eyes of this sandy blonde haired young boy looked up at me as he answered the 10 questions. He rarely took his eyes off of me as he spoke. I couldn't help but be amazed at the wisdom this young boy possessed despite the number years he had spent on this planet.

The first thing that caught my interest was the reference to him supporting his friends through their "heart attacks." When times are tough and we think the world is against us we experience a little heart attack – we experience a universal offensive that crushes our hopes and fills us with sorrow, we become heartbroken and, therefore, experience a heart attack. I get what he's saying. Many times in my life the crushing blow of some unexpected circumstance has made me feel as if I was having a heart attack. What I really enjoyed hearing Stranger 40 discuss was the difficulty of him battling between being himself and the outside pressure to be somebody else – at nine years old he is already figuring this out.

Much of my childhood, teenage, and young adult years were spent doing things that I thought others wanted me to do, fearing the consequences of not buying into somebody else's ideal of who I should be. These consequences of course were never confirmed, but it was the reality that I created inside my head. I don't think I ever visited the question of *who I was* until after high school. I had an idea of who I wanted to be – a risk taker, someone everybody likes, someone unique, a fierce entrepreneur. Never did I once think that I just wanted to be myself. The irony in all of this is that in the journey to be an inspiring unique individual I stepped on many of my values, I compromised my integrity, and I subscribed to beliefs that felt unnatural – this left me unfulfilled and seeking more temporary satisfaction.

The journey of being myself continues every day. The more I search the more I find out. The more experiences I have the more I find myself shaped and shifted. The exploration is a continuous process – a teeter-totter of personal discoveries followed by lost and hidden beliefs. Am I being myself now?

I'm learning that I'd rather have people respect me for powerfully expressing my truth than liking me when I compromise my true values. This is a tough place for me, but one I am deeply committed to. I make more decisions with my heart today than I did yesterday. This surrender to the truth inside of me has made my life more fulfilling and less of a struggle.

Being ourselves is freedom. But, we are also human – this exploration will continue as long as we live and there will be days where we feel grounded and connected to our truth followed by times of insecurity and doubt.

We will find ourselves again as long as we keep asking and answering the important questions. Because, it costs us too much to try and live the lives of others when a great life lies ahead that is fully and completely our own.

STRANGER 41

"Time is free, but it's priceless. You can't own it, but you can use it. You can't keep it, but you can spend it. Once you've lost it you can never get it back."
- Harvey MacKay

An accomplished collegiate athlete and a driven performer, she spent years working in a corporate atmosphere that was miserable. Contemplating drastic change, she never imagined she'd be in the place she is now.

My wife and I had arrived in Atlanta on a Thursday night for a four-day action packed vacation. While having dinner on the first night with friends, Erin made my jaw drop when she surprised me with second row Yo-Yo Ma tickets for the following night. I am a huge fan of Yo-Yo Ma. His passion and excellence in performing his craft as the world's top cellist leaves me in awe. Despite my high expectations, he did not disappoint.

Next big event: Touring the Atlanta Falcons football training facilities on Saturday, meeting team staff, and spending time with friends prior to stepping onto the field at the Georgia Dome before the big NFL game on Sunday night.

Close to twenty people watched the bone crushing hits and glorious displays of athleticism from a luxury suite inside the domed stadium. People milled about the suite watching, talking, eating, and cheering as the action took place down below. A young woman had just finished a conversation and was sitting alone looking out onto the field.

I walked over to her and kneeled down to make my pitch. At first she was a bit reluctant, but after a little prodding on my part, this young woman who works in high level professional sports administration agreed to be Stranger 41.

1) What is your dream job?

"I would want to be a professional soccer athlete. I'm just a competitive person and I've played soccer all my life and to be able to play at that level would be my dream job. And, because I work in professional sports and I see these players doing what they love to do and they're making money to play sports, it's just amazing."

2) What fulfills you?

"Friends and family around me. I mean, that's what makes me me. It's how I was brought up. And, the friends that I have, just them being around me, it just fills who I am."

3) What is your greatest fear?

"To be honest, dying. That is my greatest fear. Because, I don't understand. Not that I don't understand – I just don't. I know that there is heaven on earth and I just don't know what's going to go on in my life after that and to not, and for that not, to be the same as what I'm doing right now. Change – it comes down to change. That is my biggest fear."

4) What do you want more of in life?

"Time outside of work."

What would you do with it?

"Spend more time with my husband. He also works in professional sport, so we're both working a lot and generally we don't see each other a lot. And, that would be my biggest thing is I'd like to see him more, and see my family more. We have to travel to see them because they're all spread out."

5a) What is your greatest accomplishment?

"There are two things. One was playing soccer in college – collegiate soccer. Number two is where I am today. I think I've found it pretty easy through other people, but it's still a huge accomplishment for me to be where I am (in professional sport). It's pretty amazing to me. I love what I do and couldn't imagine doing anything else because I've been in the corporate world before and was miserable."

5b) What are you most ashamed of?

"I guess college. I'd like to go back and do college over again and maybe go to class a little bit more, study a little bit harder. And, just because I loved college so much, I'd love to go back again. Not that I'm ashamed of it, I'd just like to go back again."

6) What makes you sad?

"I'm a very emotional person, and death. I mean that's just what makes me sad cause you're losing someone and your losing part of yourself if they're close, if they're friends, so I mean that makes me very sad. I'm also a person who doesn't like confrontation. I mean, I don't like that and I don't like when there's something going wrong and it's on me. I just want to make it right. I don't want to be the cause of the problem."

7) What is the hardest thing you have ever experienced?

"I'm a lucky person. I've really hadn't had to go through anything, I mean, too difficult. Thankfully, I'm lucky for that. I don't know, I just think I'm a very lucky person that there's nothing, there's never been, anything extremely difficult. I've had an amazing life and there's nothing I'd really change. I think there will be because my husband and I both work with the same professional sports team and I'm sure we're not going to both want to work here for the rest of our lives. So, eventually one of us is going to have to move on and I think that is going to be a huge decision and a huge struggle. So, I know that that time is coming it just hasn't happened yet which is a good thing. You need to ask me that question after that happens."

8) What is great about you?

"I think my drive, and my competitiveness, and just my personality that I have, and how I connect with other people. I just like to listen to other people and know what's going on in their lives and why they're hurting and just being able to talk to people."

9) Who are you?

"I think it just kind of goes back to the question before. I'm competitive, driven, motivated person that I'm just gonna, my drive is to, make sure everything is perfect. I'm a perfectionist pretty much. That's just kind of who I am."

10) What question do you want to ask me now?

"Ask me if I love my job."

Do you love your job?

"I love my job. I get to meet people like you. That's why I love my job."

Imagine if we had more time. If you had a few more hours in the day, an extra day in our week, or more how would you use it? Would you do more of the same or something completely different? Would you do the things you wished you had more time to do or would those be pushed away for other "important" things, stashing them away until the time is "right"?

There is a quote by author Timothy Ferriss: "Someday is a disease that will take your dreams to the grave with you." Someday I'll try, someday I'll get to it, soon I'll do it – we all fall into this trap. If we had more time, how would we really spend it? We are masters at being *busy*, but the question is 'am I being productive or just busy'? Am I inventing things to do so that I can be busy and avoid the things I say are important?

As Ferriss says, "Our time on this earth is limited and undefined." Why do we wait for cathartic events to shock us into realigning with our true values? Our time is limited, so why do we fall into such cavalier disregard for time and allow ourselves to take for granted the things that are truly precious?

This is a life that will always be one day away from happiness.

Life is not measured by minutes but by moments. By increasing the quality of those moments, we increase the quality of our lives. Love the time in your life and how you use it. Live your dreams, love the people around you, and don't let *someday*, *tomorrow*, or *there's not enough time*, push important things or people away.

STRANGER 42

"I don't measure a man's success by how high he climbs but how high he bounces when he hits bottom."
- General George S. Patton

He fought hard to keep the tears from gushing out. A man who fought in battles across the world as an elite soldier, he was not prepared to lose his best friend.

I had failed many times to interview my Strangers early in the week in order to have ample time to write and prepare a great piece. No matter what, each week I set the intention to interview someone early but my hours and days slipped by and next thing I knew Sunday had arrived. I found myself with less than 24 hours to meet the next stranger.

I was out scouring the streets in my new hometown late on Sunday night and I thought the local tavern would be a good place to find a stranger. I envisioned cozying up to a "regular" who spent their time sipping beer and pushing the buttons on a worn down slot machine. Unfortunately, when I pulled up I could hear the bass pumping from the building and a live band was playing inside. It would have been impossible to hold an interview with booming speakers, so my next plan was to head out to a truck stop just outside of town on the highway. Hoping to find a truck driver drinking a late night coffee before heading back on the road, my next vision was the two of us sitting across from one another sharing old road stories. No luck. Finally, I headed back into town and took a shot at the hockey rink to see if there were any late night recreation league hockey players who I could grab before they went home.

I entered the doors to the large complex and it wasn't so busy. There were games going on in each of the two rinks, but really no one around in the concourse area. I lingered around until I spotted the janitor cleaning the floor and I thought I'd give him a shot, but then another man started walking in my direction. He was quite tall and had a thick build. He wore a light jacket over top of a blue Toronto Maple Leafs jersey.

Strangely, I became a bit nervous but approached him anyhow and made my pitch.

He scrunched up his face and looked at me like I was crazy. He questioned what the interview was about and I shared a little bit about the experiment and how far along it was and that he would be the 42nd person this year if he would accept. He stood there and looked down at me. After contemplating the situation, he finally agreed.

1) What is your dream job?

"In the operations planning department for NATO or UNDPKO in New York. My background is in military and those are areas that you get to go out and do some good in the world, but you do it in a proactive way instead of a wishful thinking way."

2) What fulfills you?

"I think recently I've discovered that it's family. I've got a new daughter."

3) What is your greatest fear?

"Failure. It's a measure of who you are, what you are, what you think, you believe. Failure is a big thing."

4) What do you want more of?

"Time. More of the things I want to do rather than the things I have to do."

5a) What is your greatest accomplishment?

"Staying alive. There are so many ways that I think you can fall off the rail. Right? Lots of people don't make it. Right? So, staying alive."

5b) What are you most ashamed of?

"Mistakes. A couple that were rather large areas, but that's for me to live with."

6) What makes you sad?

"Lately, just seeing instances of cruelty from person to person, especially parents that hurt kids, strangers that hurt kids. I mean, that's the thing I've noticed lately. When you see these stories about these kids where horrible things happen to them and they've done nothing other than exist all made by people who are supposed to protect them, that makes me very sad."

7) What is the hardest thing you have ever experienced?

"Strangely enough out of all the places I've been and things I've done, the hardest thing I've had to do is put my dog down. I had to lead him into a room and let someone kill him, and he trusted me. He wagged his tail when they walked in the room with the needle."

8)What is great about you?

"I think I have a lot of patience and understanding, almost too much."

9) Who are you?

"That is a very good question, and when I get the answer to that I'll probably have one foot in the grave. Who are we? The definition of life is changing. You're always growing and evolving, so I think that who you are as a function of that will change and evolve over time. At one time I was a soldier, another time I was a student, and now I'm a father. So, it depends when in my lifetime you would have asked me that question. Two, three, four years from now I may be a father and something else, so that's a good thing."

Monsters hid inside my head when I was vying for a spot on the Olympic Bobsleigh Team. For eight years these beasts raged inside my head and told me that if I failed then that made me – Jayson Krause – a failure. I accepted that proposition and spent my whole career fearing failure and the terrible things that would happen should I not live up to the expectations that lived inside my head or, worse, that I wouldn't live up to others expectations of me.

When I succeeded, I held on extremely tight to that success only to squeeze the life from it and force myself into complete disaster. My best competitive results were followed literally by crashes. When I was sitting in the bottom of the valley with no relief in sight was exactly when I seemed to emerge and perform beyond my expectations and produce brilliant results.

The difference? One was fear. The other was presence.

I remember the day it came to me, like a slap on the face. I had retired from bobsleigh and was working out with a friend of mine who is a highly decorated international athlete. We were doing bench press. I was on my last set and I couldn't push the last repetition up on the rack. I was exhausted and a bit ashamed that my strength had fallen off so quickly. My friend playfully punched me on the shoulder and said, "Perfect, you made it to failure, exactly where you want to be."

My hand smacked my forehead as I realized the self-imposed blindness I had lived with for the previous eight years. *"I made it to failure... exactly where I want to be."* The paradox of it all dawned on me.

You mean, I spent so many hours trying to achieve failure in my workouts only to fear it when it was time to perform? It makes so much sense to me now. Without failure, my muscles would never tear and rebuild themselves to be stronger. Without failure, I would not and could not improve.

Children are brilliant at failing as they learn to walk, stumbling and bumping into everything until they master the art of maneuvering. Somewhere along the road we forget what got us where we are today: failing. If we attacked failure in the area where we most wanted to grow, imagine the results we would get. We could eliminate everything that didn't work and get to the real stuff that could get us to where we need to go while providing great growth and learning along the way by making our spirits stronger and our vision greater.

Stranger 42 is right about a few things when it comes to failure: *Failure is a measure of who you are.* Without it you wouldn't be where you are now.

Failure is a big thing. In fact it's the biggest thing on the path to success. Without it you will never get there. You must fail to succeed. Celebrate failure enough and soon you'll be celebrating success.

STRANGER 43

"The way you see people is the way you treat them."
- Zig Ziglar

Just one month after celebrating their retirement, her husband was diagnosed with terminal cancer. He would last eighteen months before passing away in their home, under her loving care.

The city zoo was infested with vampires, walking bears, fairy tale princesses, and many other interesting characters. My wife and I had joined friends at an event, 'Boo at the Zoo'. The zoo had been transformed into a Halloween-themed venue for kids. Since we were going to be having one soon, we figured we'd start now by attending events like this to prepare ourselves for what lies ahead. Haunted houses, ghosts and goblins, and little kids dressed up in costumes surrounded us as we made our way around in the dark, cold evening.

Our friends have two young children, the youngest about eight months old. So after being out for about 30 minutes, we had decided to go warm up in the cafeteria, drink hot chocolate, and change a diaper.

The cafeteria was huge and there weren't many people in it, but I spotted a middle-aged woman with long brown hair sitting by herself on the other side. She had her laptop out and was eating supper. I became intrigued as it's not normal to see someone at the zoo with their laptop. I told my wife where I was headed and swept in.

The woman looked up at me, slightly embarrassed after shoving the last piece of a large hot dog into her mouth. I stood uncomfortably above her waiting for her to finish chewing before making my pitch. She sat there appearing a little suspicious and asked me more about the meaning behind 52 People. While I shared my explanation, her suspicion left as her eyes became red and teary. The blood shot instantly in and covered the whiteness around her eyes as tears started to pool and threatened to overflow.

"I will try and answer your questions. But, on November 18th, it will have been five years since my husband died from cancer."

1) What is your dream job?

"I have created my dream job. I own an LED company that supplies jumbotrons. And, I have a new partner and he's wonderful. We do things like put on Santa-Vision and Holiday Postcards for children. Part of our mandate is that we do a lot of donations. So, I'm kind of there."

2) What fulfills you?

"My new family and my family. When I'm full of life and full of love. I was alone with my husband for many years and we never had children. And, I was in the military, so I was far away from home. I was always far away from home. So, now I've moved back west and I have family. I actually have family down the street. So, I get to know my nieces that I never got to know before. That's what fulfills me is seeing family."

3) What is your greatest fear?

"Cancer, mostly, because I saw how my husband died and how much pain he was in. He was a very vibrant, vibrant man. He was a hunter. He was a forester. He's done twenty five years in the military, jumped out of planes, faced sharks. We used to scuba dive, ride motorcycles. To be diagnosed with a terminal disease so quickly and have him go in eighteen months with no hope. Mostly, it's the system itself. The healthcare system is extremely broken and they're breaking down the people within it. In my humble opinion it still has a lot further to come down before it goes back up again. So, dying in pain is my fear."

4) What do you want more of in life?

"Free time."

What would you do with it?

"Clean my house, although no one has ever had written on their tombstone that she was a really great housekeeper. I'd like to spend some more time with my mother, although I do spend at least a month a year with her. I had her for six months after my husband passed away and, I, I truly cherished the time in getting to know her as an adult and as a woman. I would spend more time with my family. It's the only thing that is forever."

5a) What is your greatest accomplishment?

"I did twenty three years in the Air Force and am very proud of my service time. I wouldn't do anymore because I was pretty tired then too. But, after I retired from the Air Force, a month after that, was when my husband was diagnosed with terminal cancer and I took care of him and I kept him at home and he passed away in our home and not in a hospital – and I'm proud of that, but it's still hard. So, I've done a lot of things that I am proud of. Serving my country was something that I truly enjoyed. And, then being able to give that gift to (my husband) I enjoyed that also. Still tough though."

5b) What are you most ashamed of?

"The way I treated the people that I vowed to love, honor, and cherish at times. Stupidity gets in the way, it always will."

6) What makes you sad?

"Well, I probably still have a lot of sadness left in my, in my life. Children hurting and animals hurting, and the way that we treat each other. The way that we treat each other in life horrifies me. Whether it's the Jewish Holocaust or whether or not it's people floating down the river in Haiti and Somalia, or in Iran or Iraq. The way we treat each other as human beings. We are horribly cruel to each other."

7) What is the hardest thing you have ever experienced?

"Probably the death of my husband. To see the disease ravage him so quickly, you know. My father died from a disease called Huntington's disease and to see him die so slowly. And my brother has Huntington's disease and he has three young children – well they're not anymore, they're in college now. He has the same disease and he's forty-three and he's in long term care for the rest of his life. So, to watch him die very slowly is also hard. So, now I forgot what the question was. The hardest thing? The hardest thing is to watch the people around me die."

8) What is great about you?

"Funny, I had an email come around the other day and you had to list five things – from some of my friends. There (are) five of us. We were in boot camp together thirty years ago and we are still in contact. I can do long term relationships. So, I had to write these things down there too. I think the biggest thing is I'm strong. When faced with something, I'll get through it. I think that because I'm strong I'm also reliable. I'm a pretty tough cookie."

9) Who are you?

"I am middle aged woman that has the mind of an eighteen year old and can't believe that things are falling out, falling off, or falling down. And I'm a good person, and I will continue to improve on that and be a better person. So who am I? I guess I'm just a person who's trying to do right for myself, to take care of myself and my family, and not make too many more mistakes."

10) What question do you want me to ask you now?

"Am I happy?"

Are you happy?

"Yeah, I think so. I'm satisfied. Life has changed, and I seem to reinvent myself every fifteen years. So, now I am a businesswoman and for now that is OK."

Stranger 43 spoke about the way people treat one another as what makes her most sad. As a former military personnel, she had experienced harrowing sights – crimes against humanity in nations across the world. She saw the way people treat one another for the way they look, talk, pray, and live. "The way that we treat each other in life horrifies me."

We as humans can treat each other in the most heartless manner. You and I have been guilty of the same thing, much like stranger 43 when she spoke about what she was most ashamed of. "The way I treated the people that I vowed to love, honor, and cherish at times. Stupidity gets in the way... it always will."

"Stupidity gets in the way" is one way to look at it, but the bigger picture is that we get in the way. Why do people treat others poorly? Why do people cause others harm? It has nothing to do with them; it has everything to do with us.

Have you ever treated someone with contempt when your heart was full of happiness and love? Have you ever intentionally hurt someone physically or emotionally when you were full of compassion? It is so easy to point to the wrong doings of others and find reasons to dislike, hate, and bully.

What eyes are you looking with? We can be masters at hiding inside our heads and inside our own world. Living with anger, fear, and consumed by sorrow, we become blind. When we become blind we react by treating everything like objects – lashing out on the things that trigger us. We put people in a labeled box: *race*, *idiot*, or anywhere we can lay blame. The boxes help us run away from the reality that the turmoil is within us and has nothing to do with them.

In those moments when we are at peace with ourselves the veils seem to drop and we temporarily see the ones around us as equals. We see them as individuals who possess both pain and suffering and joy and happiness. We see them as those who desire to express themselves in their life and continue along their path. The way we see people is the way we treat them. Although our eyes sit inside the mindless chatter of our heads, we tend to forget that our eyes are still connected to our hearts.

STRANGER 44

"The closest to being in control we will ever be is in that moment that we realize we're not."
- Brian Kessler

He grew up in a family of engineers where everything is calculated and exact – straight lines and answers. What happens in the heat of the moment when a dying woman is lying unsuspectingly in front of you and your calculations can't help you?

I stopped at the Road King truck stop where close to a hundred large semi trucks sat idling but few bodies were around. I approached one man who flashed a toothless smile and wore a rolled up beanie, as he stared upward at an elevated television screen. We made pleasant small talk before I made my pitch. Once I made my pitch his demeanor changed and he looked at me threateningly, "Don't waste your time, get out of here!"

I heeded his advice and headed back for my car holding a second location in mind.

Lights flashed and bells rang as I walked along the casino floor, stopping periodically to watch a roll of the dice, a flip of the card, or the push of a button. Despite it being an early Sunday evening, the place was bustling. I thought about approaching someone at the slot machines, so I trolled the area waiting to catch someone's eye. I trolled to no avail, as people locked on to the screen and intently focused while the "bells, cherries, and sevens" spun round and round.

I ended up in the palace of sensory overload and had become a bit discouraged at the opportunity to find someone. I was so discouraged that I had thrown in the towel and figured it just wasn't going to happen. I exited the warmth of the casino and spotted a large man smoking just outside of the doors. He was about 6-foot-3 with short dark hair and broad shoulders. The dark puffy jacket he wore made his broad shoulders look even larger. Despite the intimidating image, I approached and met a 27-year-old man who had recently moved across the country looking for work.

1) What is your dream job?

"Teacher. I've always wanted to be a teacher. I enjoy helping little kids. Like, I would like to be a grade school teacher."

2) What fulfills you?

"I guess it's changed since recently because I've moved away from all my family. But, being with family on the weekends. Things like that. That's most fulfilling for me and I haven't been able to it in eight months because I moved out here."

3) What is your greatest fear?

"Fire. I hate it. I don't know, I can't control it. I'm a control freak."

4) What do you want more of in life?

"Money. Travel more. Be more. I don't know, I just think life is stressful without it."

5a) What is your greatest accomplishment?

"Completing my engineering degree definitely was. I come from a family of engineers and my brothers and sisters that are older than me are engineers and my parents are engineers and I was the one they didn't think would do it. That would definitely be it. I dropped out originally and went back. So, it was like a, you know what I mean, 'you couldn't do it' type of thing, and I said, 'Ok I'll show you.' Then did it."

5b) What are you most ashamed of?

"Since it's anonymous, I guess it was a failed engagement. I was engaged. I was the reason for the failure, so that was definitely a letdown."

6) What makes you sad?

"I don't like to see people, like needy people. That really makes me sad. You know what I mean? I don't feel as if, I feel like there's so much surplus in terms of money and all these people. I hate seeing that. It really bothers me. You know what I mean? That bothers me."

7) What is the hardest thing you have ever experienced?

"I watched a lady die, so that was a tough one. She fell off a roof and I was kind of nearby being helpless. I'm not a doctor, nor do I know what to do – just in that sense, being helpless. Just kind of having to be there and not being able to do anything. Like I told you before, I'm kind of a control freak and being in a situation that you can't control is not a real good feeling."

8) What is great about you?

"I look mean. Like, I look big, tough guy, mean guy, but I guess I'm really actually gentle in terms of my compassion towards other people. So, that's probably the best thing about me. People don't expect it. You know what I mean? So, when they see it it's kind of a shock to them."

9) Who are you?

"I can only tell you my attributes. I'm just a hard working guy. Kind guy looking out for people. Always trying to do what's best for everyone in that sense. Family oriented."

There is a fable titled "Maybe, maybe not" and it goes something like this:

There is an old man who lives with his son on a farm, and one day their horse escapes and is nowhere to be found. The people in the town say,

"You are the unluckiest man around."

The man replies, "Maybe, maybe not."

The following day the man's missing horse returns and has brought with him four wild horses that join him in the stable. Upon seeing the man's new found horses, the townspeople say,

"You are the luckiest man around!"

To which the man replies, "Maybe, maybe not."

The following day the man's son is breaking one of the new wild horses and gets bucked off and suffers a broken leg. As a result of his son's injury the old man is forced to do all of the farm work alone. The townspeople say,

"You are the unluckiest man around."

To which the man replies, "Maybe, maybe not."

The next day there's a knock on the door. It was a military official conscripting new soldiers

to invade the neighboring country. The man's son
was spared from conscription because of his
broken leg. The townspeople said,
    "You are the luckiest man around."
    To which he replied, "Maybe, maybe
not".... and so the story goes.

The man in this story shows great wisdom in the area of surrender – the place of working hard in his daily life for the things he wants and needs, but not falling victim to believing he can control the outcomes.

Stranger 44 could have studied medicine for years and still not have been able to save the woman who fell from her roof. You can spend years building a seemingly impenetrable defense system of trenches only to have your attackers fly over them. You cannot control outcomes only your efforts.

The old man in the story has surrendered to the unfolding of his life. The surrender is not a lying down, giving up type of surrender but a surrender of wisdom. He was a man who knew how to accept the things he could not change.

We are not in control of our outcomes. The moment when we think we have it and we double down in life - the dealer flips a jack and the house wins.

STRANGER 45

"I'm not supposed to love you. I'm not supposed to care. I'm not supposed to live my life wishing you were there. I'm not supposed to wonder where you are or what you do...I'm sorry I can't help myself, I'm in love with you.*"*
- Unknown

Imagine thinking differently from everyone else. Imagine waking up in the morning and seeing what other people don't and feeling something strong driving you in a different direction. Very few people have the courage to take a leap of faith and follow their hearts. Sometimes a leap of faith is all it takes. A leap of faith and a guardian angel.

I briskly walked through the empty hallway. My steps echoed as my pace quickened, hoping to make it in before class started. As I arrived at classroom I found the thick wooden door to be locked. I peered through the window to find every seat occupied by curious students. Out of luck? Not quite. Another workshop was just closing its door. I ran over and grabbed the handle before the door closed on me and quickly took my seat in a vacant desk in the back row.

I was in the Rocky Mountains in the beautiful city of Canmore. Erin was volunteering at a non-profit booth at the LifeFest – a weekend festival promoting health, healing, and the environment. While she volunteered, I participated in workshops throughout the day. The workshop I was late for and never got in: *Secrets to increase your energy.* The workshop I ended up at in the last minute: *Connecting with your healing angels.* Although it wasn't what I had expected to attend, I accepted that the universe put me there for a reason.

While I sat in the back of the room, I watched the young woman, about 30 years old, discuss the theories of angel communication and how you can apply it to your life. While she spoke, I became intrigued about her life and how someone gets into the industry of angel communication. So, after the workshop I walked around the hallways until I spotted her. I pounced on the opportunity to interview her.

1) What is your dream job?

"An author – sharing my work with the world. Basically, really trying to connect with people on a much broader basis than I am able to now. And, I'm working on it. I'm getting there."

2) What fulfills you?

"Passion. You need to have passion in life. Just living each moment in the present – right now. Not worrying about the past. Not worrying about the future. Just being here, being alive, being open. Just experiencing all that life has to offer and being passionate about what you do."

3) What is your greatest fear?

"Probably not to be able to do what I love to do. Not to be able to connect with people anymore. Just a couple of years ago I was working in the corporate world and I was very shut off and I just felt like I was going through the day-to-day motions, not really living, not experiencing anything. So now what I do is I connect with people. I actually get to help them. I get to make their lives better. For me, not being able to do that anymore is very frightening."

4) What do you want more of in life?

"Friends. More connection with people. The more friends that you can have – and I don't mean acquaintances, close friends – just the more that you can invite them into experiences with you and you can experience their experiences and you can share."

5a) What is your greatest accomplishment?

"Becoming who I am. It has taken a lot of courage to step out and actually admit to the world what I do and what my gifts are. So, that would be my greatest accomplishment, saying, 'Here I am. If you like me, you like me. If you don't, you don't."

5b) What are you most ashamed of?

"Probably the fact that I'm not able to completely be myself around some people. And, I know it's not necessarily anything to do with me. It's just that they can't accept me yet and I'm just waiting for the opportunity when they get there. 'Ok I'm still me, I may have changed my profession, I may have opened up a lot, but I'm still the same person.'"

6) What makes you sad?

"Cruelty, especially with animals. It's so funny, one of my friends actually thinks that I'm a little bit weird because of this, but if I see an animal getting hurt or abused it affects me way more than if it's a person. It just makes me sad, especially when people intentionally do it."

7) What is the hardest thing you have ever experienced?

"Probably coming here, starting my own business – completely new. I knew one person in the area, right, like that's it. I basically said, 'Ok, I'm giving up everything that I've built in my hometown. I'm giving up my life out there, coming here, and building completely from scratch.' But, it's been good."

8) What is great about you?

"Probably my compassion. I really truly want to help people and make a difference in their lives."

9) Who are you?

"I'm just a person who has had the opportunity to experience some pretty great stuff. I'm a normal person who sees extraordinary things."

There is a powerful force that is against us. Some call it social hypnosis. Others may call it homeostasis, or the virus of the mind. This force tells us what we should do, who we should be, what we should think, and, most importantly, not to accept ourselves if we are different. This force tells us how to spend money, how to spend time, and how to go through the routines of our lives. This force tries relentlessly to numb our senses and passions and will push us to fit tightly into a box with the rest of the boxes, stacked neatly to the side one on top of another. The force is so powerful in its attempts to indoctrinate us.

You're crazy if you think you can do that.

It's too risky.

It's a safer bet if you do it this way.

If you make this decision you will be left alone.

That never works out.

Unrealistic.

This makes more sense.

This force whispers to us, and these internal voices aren't the only way we are forced to think small. Television, magazines, and the internet strive to prove we aren't beautiful enough, smart enough, nor have the resources to do it. They tell us the way it "should" be done. They tell us that if we were able to do it, we would have already done it –just like the overnight successes we see. This force hates change or any deviation from its plan to keep us as small cookie cutter humans.

The decision to emerge from this force is the ultimate expression of self love. It is the place of coming home to what feels right to you. It is the aliveness of meeting your true self for the first time outside of the box, unwrapped, and ready to experience the playful and authentic nature of your true gifts. When we emerge and truly accept our abilities, we experience butterflies, passion, and the experience of meeting our true soul mate – the one who was kept hidden from us for most of our lives.

Like Stranger 45, there comes a point in our lives when leaving our natural gifts unused is a far greater risk to ourselves than boldly stepping into the fear of criticism and judgment. Once we emerge and get a taste of the powerful expression inside of us, we can't help but fall in love with who we truly are.

STRANGER 46

"Man, alone, has the power to transform his thoughts into physical reality; man, alone, can dream and make his dreams come true."
- Napoleon Hill

A decision must be made – a decision that will forever change his life.

The days varied between bright sunny days, misty dreariness, and full out torrential downpours. I was back in Northern California, deep in the Redwood Forest, studying arcs, failure, space, and particles all in the context of developing Co-active™ leadership.

During the five day retreat, I had been in the presence of an alchemist and never realized it until the last day. This alchemist had long hair that had once been black but was now taken over with mostly grey. His smooth dark complexion showed his rich Mexican heritage and his face scrunched up with a beaming smile whenever he walked through the lodge.

All week he had dazzled the group with his ability to roll our eyes into the back of our heads with the rich taste of his culinary creations. It was the last day, however, that gave me the urge to approach him for an interview. He emerged from the kitchen, tossed his apron to the side, and had a seat at the piano. The walls of the lodge echoed with his impassioned performance as he closed his eyes, put his fingers against the ivory white keys, and created music. Meet Stranger 46, an alchemist in every sense.

1) What is you your dream job?

"Being a practicing, well-paid musician and/or chef. Musician would probably be it. It's the connection between waking and dreaming. It's the connection between physical and spiritual. It's the connection between earth and heaven. It's the conduit between that. It's something that's a gift, and it was a gift that was given to me in the crib. As my teacher would say, and as Red Skelton would say, 'If you have a gift, it's from God and if you use your gift, it's a gift to God.' So, I want to be able to use my gift. And, I discover when I play music for people it lights them up. The world is full of people who are full of hardship and sorrow and angst, and if I could play something to get people walking out of the room with a smile on their face, or feed people and walk out with a smile on their face and nourish them and support them, then it's all good. You know? And then, if I could support myself in the whole process that's even better yet – icing on the cake."

2) What fulfills you?

"Being full of life and being loved. Love and being loved. That's the ultimate for me –loving and being loved."

3) What is your greatest fear?

"Not being totally accepted for who I am. I'm not exactly quite the mold of most people – which a lot of people don't realize which I'll tell you right now – since I'm kind of coming out with it. I'm actually, for a lack of a better word, a transgendered person. So, I'm actually transitioning at this moment more into my female side. So, that's been a path I've been on since I've been, like, five and I've only really been assertively manifesting more within the last nine years. More specifically, in the last year and half (I) really accelerated it up. And so I'm really kind of afraid that those people I 'come out' to aren't going to quite get it because it's not been given a lot of good promo through years and I think a lot of people don't quite understand it. And, I'm actually trying to come and understand it a bit myself even though I'm part of that whole process. That's probably my greatest fear. I just like to be me and express who I am."

4) What do you want more of in life?

"That could go in different levels. The top of the line is probably love and be loved – that's it. Love and be loved – that's it."

5a) What is your greatest accomplishment?

"I don't know if I have a greatest accomplishment yet. My greatest accomplishment I think probably for me at this point in my life – Well, it's not the money thing that's for sure – probably having spent the earlier part of my life actually traveling and seeing the world and other people and other cultures and getting a lot of education that way. So, life experience."

5b) What are you most ashamed of?

"Probably being a procrastinator. Of not stepping up in moments when I should have stepped up or either being too lazy or not following through on projects or just being a procrastinator. It's really a drag because it stifles my own development and evolution."

6) What makes you sad?

"Humanities inhumanity to humanity and how people can treat people so cruelly. People who can't see the divinity within each person that we all are and people who can't realize the God within all of us. People treat people like crap, like less than animals and less than shit. It makes me sad because it's such a waste of beauty, in behalf of the person who is laying it out and in behalf of the person who is receiving that kind of crap. So, that really makes me sad to see that people treat each other unjustly. And, how living in a world where we have such a great wealth and people are so poor and untaken care of, that really breaks my heart."

7) What is the hardest thing you have ever experienced?

"Losing people I love. My mom, my dad. (In) 1996 I lost my mother, my father, my step father, two of my aunts, and two of my cousins and that was just in one year. So, the hardest thing for me is losing people I love on the planet who have been so integral in my life and knowing that – in least as far as this lifetime goes – I'll never see them again, though I carry pieces of them with me in the fabric of my own existence. That's the hardest thing is losing people I love."

8) What is great about you?

"The ability to always be on the sunny side of life. I always seem to be happy person for the most part. When I apply myself, my creativity is really great. What's the question, what's great about me? Wow. When I'm working on all cylinders and focused. God that's a hard question for me because, I don't know, maybe I don't have enough self esteem in myself, I don't know. Probably though – when I got my shit together – probably being the creative person I am and being the artist that I am is the most greatest thing, the goodest thing, about me. I guess my creativity is the greatest thing about me when I'm applying it and actually functioning correctly with it."

9) Who are you?

"I am that I am. I am the breath of God, I'm the eternal rolling divinity that is. I am a creative soul. I am an artist. I am a spirit trying to evolve. I'm trying to. I'm the prodigal child trying to get back to the home, to the God, to the integration of myself of the realization of that that's greater than me. I'm questing. I'm a soul journeyer. I'm the brother. I'm the sister. I'm the uncle."

Transformation is happening everywhere. Every moment something is changing. Most of these changes occur without notice. They fly past us quickly, darting from here to there, altering the states around them, hidden from our sight. Many of these changes are occurring inside our bodies and we don't even notice them.

What exactly was it that transformed me at different times in my life from a laughing, happy, abundant person into a fearful, hoarder living in scarcity? I don't know. What exactly was it that transformed me from being in a mental movie inside my head into a present state where my senses became alive? It was alchemy.

An alchemist is a master of transformation, someone who blends elements and creates desired change. An alchemist is someone who uses tools to give life to something. We are surrounded by alchemy. The alchemist blends vision with effort to produce the house we live in. The alchemist gathers vision and a brush to inspire us with the art that brings life to the wall it hangs on. Our toes have tapped to the alchemy of poetry blended with music and our bodies have felt the soul in the alchemical powers of the chef who created a dance between spices, meat, vegetables, and fire. We are surrounded by these masters everywhere.

The problem is that many unconscious alchemists selfishly transform things into chaos and attempt to push the transformation into a downward spiral. They unconsciously create an impact that is damaging and don't realize that they are the ones responsible. What are you responsible for transforming? A frown into a smile? A trusting person into one in agony?

Stranger 47 is an alchemist in every sense – creating in the kitchen and taking people on a journey through food, putting his fingers to ivory and moving their souls through music, and putting his thoughts and dreams into action to create a complete physical transformation within himself.

It takes passion, vision, curiosity and courage to choose purposeful transformation. Understand that we are all alchemists and that we can choose our impact at any moment in time. What will you blend together to transform? Blend your ideas and actions into the world and transform the experiences of your life into gold.

STRANGER 47

"If I have seen further than others, it is by standing upon the shoulders of giants."
- Isaac Newton

In times like this, she wants to turn to someone. Dad? No, he's long gone. Mom? No, she's either high on drugs or still in jail. Who to turn to? She turns to her little brother and whispers in his ear, "I'll take care of you."

High-school presents many challenges. Being a teenager can be tough. Learning new responsibilities, experiencing peer pressures, and striving for good grades and social acceptance can be a full time job. Now, imagine being 17 years old with a mother who was a drug addict and was in and out of jail and a father who was rarely, if ever, around. Imagine being 17 years old and having the responsibility of not only raising yourself but taking the responsibility of raising your ten year old sibling.

I was speaking at an athletic awards banquet on a Wednesday night. The theme was about lies, labels, and failures. There was another speaker who was a seventeen-year-old high-school student. She was also a role model, volleyball player, big sister, and hero who inspired me and over 100 others with her story about perseverance and perspectives. She also became Stranger 47.

1) What is your dream job?

"To be a paramedic – the adrenalin rush, the passion I have for it, the want, and just to be able to say I did something for everybody or society."

2) What fulfills you?

"I like to help people. I think that the feeling of doing something good makes you feel like you're on top of the world. And, I feel like I get happy through music and that's what makes me happy."

3) What is your greatest fear?

"My greatest fear is that I won't follow through with my dreams or, like, something will stop me from fulfilling my dreams and making me happy. Because my mom has definitely done a lot of bad, negative things to me in my life, I want to show people that just because bad things happened that you can still fulfill your dreams and nothing is going to stop you. So, I hope that nothing in life ever stops me from doing what I want to do."

4) What do you want more of in life?

"I want more of people knowing the true things in life, not (meaningless conversation). People knowing that there's people that die every day and don't take advantage of one day. You know? Every day is precious to you and I want people to know that there's more to life than gossip, shopping, and money and life actually does count."

5a) What is your greatest accomplishment?

"My greatest accomplishment is getting over my childhood and being able to move past that and not fear in it anymore."

5b) What are you most ashamed of?

"I'm most ashamed that I haven't tried every day. And, some days I do get caught up in the bull crap. And, some days you just let yourself go and then you sit back and you think, 'Why did I do that today' or 'Why did I say that today?' At the end of the day I just kind of pretend that I'm talking to my grandpa and I just say sorry for letting stuff get over your head and not realizing that your caught up in the moment and not doing the right thing."

6) What makes you sad?

"What makes me sad is that there are people like robbers, rapists, murderers, they all are taking advantage of life. And then, I have my grandpa who was a really great man and he died. And, it really hurts to see that people are taking advantage of life and making themselves do these bad things and innocent people have to die."

7) What is the hardest thing you have ever experienced?

"Hardest thing I've ever had to experience is the day my grandpa died. He reached out to me and one of his last words were 'I love you princess' and then he said I love you to my grandma and he died. The hardest thing wasn't the dying part it was the part where they had to remove his body from my house and that kind of finalized that he's not longer there in the house anymore. That was the hardest part because that's actually when I felt like I said goodbye. I didn't say goodbye when he was alive. It was actually when he was leaving."

8) What is great about you?

"I think what's great about me is that I persevere from things and I always try to be optimistic. I always try to see a different side. I don't let things get to me. I always just strive for 'well what can I do to fix that.' I always try to find a solution and it's finding a positive solution."

9) Who are you?

"I'm someone that people can turn to. I'm someone who wants to make an impact and I'm someone who can make a difference."

10) What question do you want me to ask you now?

"I want you to ask me how I do it – how do I stay positive"

How do you do it – how do you stay positive?

"I think about the people that have helped me in my life. I think about the people who have made it possible for me to be who I am and I think about the people who have lost their lives for me, like your friend and my grandpa. And, I think about those people who have made a difference. And so, if they have made a difference in me, I can make a difference in someone else."

There were common messages in the speeches given by Stranger 47 and myself, although they were woven in different fabric. Her story was about family adversity and death. My story was one of adversity through sport and life. We shared our separate tales with the audience and near the end of our respective speeches the messages converged: choose your experience.

She spoke about choosing if you want to be positive or negative when faced with adversities in life – making the best of a bad situation. Mine was similar: having a choice when faced with failure. Either sulk and lament about your tarnished reputation and what was lost or step up to the challenge and change what needs to be changed to strengthen yourself moving forward – better preparing you for your next battle.

It comes down to choice. Adversity is what strengthens our soul. Adversity is the large obstacle that lies in front of us that we can run from, stare at, or climb. Setbacks are the switch-backs that allow us to climb higher and see better perspectives, develop better insight, and see further than we saw before.

This week I met a young hero who reminded me about a Norwegian tale:

> *The hero comes to a crossroads where there are three signs: "She who travels down this road will return unharmed," "She who travels down this path may or may not return," and "She who travels here will never return." Of course she chose the third.*
>
> *– Laura Sims*

Choose your path and don't look back. Look ahead and let those setbacks be switch-backs that lead you to the vista where you can stand on the shoulders of giants and see further than you have ever seen before.

STRANGER 48

"On life's vast ocean diversely we sail. Reason the card, but passion is the gale"
- Alexander Pope

Some travel large distances in life – while others not too far. Some desire to become doctors, lawyers, or athletes– while others yearn to become mermaids.

The wind blew the snow viciously across the highways making it almost impossible to see the road or any of the vehicles that traveled in front of us. As we made our way to the airport, we crossed our fingers that our flight would be able to take off and we could escape the windy frozen tundra and seek refuge down south. The warmth and beauty of the Everglades and the Gulf of Mexico awaited us, just on the north side of Tampa Bay.

After a long day of travel, we found our way to a house situated on a fresh water canal that connected to the gulf. The next morning I was feeling a slight amount of guilt for the people stuck up in the land of winter. But, I went to the beach to relax and enjoy the weather that was quickly climbing up to 80 degrees.

The smooth white sand beaches had pockets of people laying out soaking up the rays of the sun and I figured one of them would be the next Stranger.

I noticed one woman who was sitting against a rail, beside her assisted walking apparatus, looking out at the ocean. I became curious and was soon speaking with the 47 year old woman as I knelt in the sand. I had already seen the storks and read about the manatees, but this was the first time I had ever encountered a mermaid.

1) What is your dream job?

"Well, I had a great job inside sales. I made good money. I went to Europe about three times a year. I loved the job but the boss was totally unreasonable. He tried to... oh that's not the question. I would have a job where I travel a lot, inside sales, make a lot of money, and like the people I work with."

2) What fulfills you?

"Health, friendship, financial security, the health of my family."

3) What is your greatest fear?

"Well, right now I'm suffering from a broken leg recovering. So, I would say my greatest fear right now is falling again."

4) What do you want more of in life?

"Lots of things: More health, more time with my family, more money. Right now I would be out there swimming, I would be jogging, working out more, traveling more, shopping more."

5a) What is your greatest accomplishment?

"I guess my BA degree. I worked full time and went to school full time and put myself through school. So, I felt like I accomplished a lot. I didn't ask my parents for a dime. I worked during the week and went to school on the weekends."

5b) What are you most ashamed of?

"Drinking too much and making a fool of myself."

6) What makes you sad?

"Well, I'm a Christian and it makes me sad when I see other people being hurt because I feel sorry for victims. And, I pray for them."

7) What is the hardest thing you have ever experienced?

"Well, this is silly but, I was a mermaid (underwater performer) when I was eighteen (years old) and going down that tube and out into the spring I was scared. But, my fear didn't last long – just a couple of days. Getting used to that air hose back then we were really really busy, six shows a day, every day. When you are under water breathing through an air hose and when you breathe in the water goes in your nose sometimes and it's scary."

8) What is great about you?

"I'm honest. A good person. People say I'm a good friend and hard working."

9) Who are you?

"I'm a girl, or a woman, who left Ohio and came to Florida when she was eighteen to be a mermaid."

One of my favorite videos is the speech by Steve Jobs, co-founder and CEO of Apple, when he addresses the Stanford graduating class. Having never graduated from university, he stood up before the large crowd and told the story that he could relate to graduating from Stanford. He shared his tale of creating Apple, losing his job with Apple, coming back to Apple, and his unwavering passion that sustained him throughout the entire journey.

He was shocked when he was fired from his position from the company he co-created. He experienced grief and disbelief until he realized that nothing was actually taken from him. He still possessed the same amount of passion for his work, despite working with Apple or not. He simply kept moving and creating. The next company he started and built was purchased by Apple and he climbed back up the ladder to the position he occupies currently – the CEO of the company he started, got fired from, and returned to.

We experience many different events in our lives that shape us and shift us onto new paths. Places we never imagined suddenly appear before us, and unexpected disasters rear their ugly heads at the most inopportune times. We often respond to these decisions by making the reasonable choice – the one that seems safe or makes sense. There are also times when we choose to commit to our dreams, to commit to our passions. When we step forward into our passion we create a powerful movement that sweeps us up and carries us far and high. The passion can lift us up and remove us from the darkness that surrounds us. Passion carries us through the milky white clouds and across great lands where we can dive into the flesh of the ocean and transform into whatever we desire. We can remove the barriers that impede our movement and learn to dance with the dolphins and perform beneath the sea.

STRANGER 49

"When I grow up I want to be a little boy."
- Joseph Heller

At three years old, he understands what most of us struggle our whole lives to figure out.

On a seaside porch, I sat in the Everglades. River otters swam about, chasing the abundance of fish in the water. A light mist hovered over top the ground despite the warm sun.

Stranger 49 sat near me. He was working away. I wanted to approach and interview him, but I was concerned about distracting him from his work. Instead, I watched and waited. Completely immersed in his craft – shaping, sculpting and creating – he used his tools to cut and carve with precision. As he completed each segment, he would delicately set each one aside and continue working away.

The clouds snuck over the sun creating brief shade and a moment for me to swoop in. Stranger 49 lifted his head and looked at the sky before glancing over at me and smiling. I smiled back and pulled out my recorder and scooted a chair beside him.

His parents sat on the deck below, sipping their coffee and casually looking up to see their 3-year-old. Stranger 49 spent the next moments scrunching his forehead and thinking hard about the questions I asked him while he worked on his play-dough.

1) What is your dream job?

"Hibernating."

2) What fulfills you?

"Finding a file phone. It's about play-dough. Making out of a castle block."

3) What is your greatest fear?

"I am scared of the dark – the monsters in the dark. That's just that I want somebody to stay with me and sleep with me. (My grandpa) always does that, but he doesn't do that very often. And, I'm scared of sharks and whales. And, I'm scared of crocodiles. I'm just worried that they could eat me all up."

4) What do you want more of in life?

"Table? I could run around it and play play-dough on it. And I could make juice on it."

5a) What is your greatest accomplishment?

"Making play-dough and play with it."

5b) What are you most ashamed of?

"Crabs and lobsters. I went to Red Lobster and I don't love lobsters and crabs and I don't love about sharks and whales."

6) What makes you sad?

"When I get a time out. I say, 'Don't forget about me,' sometimes. And, 'if they don't break mine heart,' sometimes. And, sometimes I say, 'please don't warn me to go home and have some breakfast.' But, we don't do that really often."

7) What is the hardest thing you have ever experienced?

"Make a castle out of play-dough and a clown. I'm doing right now.

What makes it hard?

"I just don't know how to do it."

8) What is great about you?

"I lost it in mine head."

What is great about you?

"I lost those things in my head also. I lost it."

9) Who are you?

"My name is Chad and I do lots of fun things with somebody and I'm scared of the dark and I'm afraid of monsters."

10) What question do you want me to ask you now?

"Hibernating?"

———————

Chad immediately turned back to his own world of playful communication with his play dough – sculpting, creating a mess and rebuilding, admiring the mess as much as the product, not judging or caring, just admiring.

The world of a three year old, revealed in the answers given, are a great reminder of what we knew then and what we know now.

For example, hibernating: the place of retirement, of rejuvenation during the cold wintery moments. To be in a place of peace, warmth, and stillness is what many people strive for as they live their current lives. They work around the clock so that they may one day hibernate.

Another answer: fear of the darkness and the monsters that reside in it –metaphorical and real. So much hides in the depths of the darkness throughout our world.

What do we want more in life? A table. Yes, a platform and structure for which we can play, build, and create. In our adult lives, we push the most meaningful things into a space of "not enough time" and not urgent or important. What we need and want is a structure for having space to play, build, and create something in our lives.

Greatest accomplishment? Committing to do something and following through with it in a playful manner, allowing ourselves to get messy with what we want to do. We can roll the dough through our hands without the imprisonment of expectations. What an accomplishment! When was the last time we all did that?

Most ashamed of? Doing things we know we don't like doing, but doing them anyhow. If you don't like crabs and lobsters, don't eat at Red Lobster. So simple.

Hardest thing to experience? Executing our vision when we don't know what the first step is. It is so easy to get stuck in the beauty of what floats in the clouds of our minds. Taking the first step to make that vision a reality when we have no clue how can be paralyzing. The first step though is rolling out the play-dough.

What is great about us? We know it and feel it at times albeit fleeting moments. Our greatness and belief in ourselves often gets stuck somewhere in the back of our minds. It builds a home there and develops agoraphobia – feeling anxious about peeking out. But, it's in there somewhere. We have to start developing the muscle of owning our greatness, otherwise it gets pushed away at a very young age.

Who am I? I am what I am. I'm not going to lie and just tell you how it is. I like to play, and when I'm not playing there's a lot of stuff out there that scares me. How grand the world would be if we were all this honest about our truth.

There is a beauty in the innocence and ignorance that a young child lives in – a truth that has no fancy wrapping. Soon this ignorance and innocence will be faced with the world of pain and judgment and walls will start to be constructed. Mistrust and doubt will creep in as the child learns that the world can be a dangerous and threatening place. The life transformed from trusting to doubting will eventually come full circle. When the horizon of our life is upon us, the wisdom returns home like a carrier pigeon that brings back the message of a meaningful life and the playfulness of a young child.

STRANGER 50

"Time heals what reason cannot."
- Seneca

She is close to ninety years old and sees the world in a completely different way. Joyful, witty and optimistic, she lived a life filled with physical and sexual abuse, abortion, and tragic death. She wonders about how she got to where she did and how one simple decision could have ended everything for her and her family.

I hung up the telephone excited and pleased with the outcome of my request. While visiting my wife's family during the Christmas holidays, I called a local senior's living complex to request permission to come down and interview one of its residents. I wanted to do something a little different. I always thought an "old folks" home would be a place that could provide a wealth of stories and experiences. The administrator gladly accepted my request and 24 hours later I was sitting in the activity room facing a woman encroaching on her ninth decade.

She slowly walked into the room. Like an inch-worm, she moved her walker forward then shuffled her feet behind it and gained ground slowly but surely. Her face was kind and her eyes avoided me at first. The uncertainty of who I was and what I was here for was written all over her.

We made small talk as she told me about her boyfriend who lives down the hall then about her heart attack that she experienced in the middle part of the year. Her head rocked back and forth in a continuous rhythm, a result of tremors that have remained with her since the heart attack. After a few more minutes of friendly chat, we dove into the ten questions.

1) What is your dream job?

"God, I don't know. The only job I did was head housekeeper of a place. I enjoyed that."

Ever dream of anything else?

"Nope, never. Maybe just meeting a man and falling in love."

2) What fulfills you?

"A hug and a kiss. Sex, but they're all too old here."

3) What is your greatest fear?

"Well, truthfully it's falling. I'm scared of falling because then you're walking around, pushed around in a wheelchair for the rest of your life. I'm afraid of water. I have a bath at night but I don't stay in for very darn long. Well, I think years ago, we had a little puddle and water there in Saskatchewan and Mom would say, 'Don't go near the water, you'll drown.'"

4) What do you want more of in life?

"The main thing is my health. I've got enough money to keep me going. I've got enough children or grandchildren. It would be nice to have a place of your own. I'm not used to being waited on; I'm independent."

5a) What is your greatest accomplishment?

"I'll tell you what. When my husband died, I used to sit and play piano songs and stuff. I made up a poem and was very proud of it. Can I recite it for you?

> *It's 18 weeks ago tonight since you went away*
> *And darling how I miss you is more than I can say*
> *I think about you every night wondering where you could be*
> *I know I'd be so happy if you were here with me*
> *You worked so hard all your life trying to get ahead*
> *and now that we could enjoy ourselves, my darling you are dead*
> *I'm looking after Fergie, he's being a pretty good cat*
> *I know he misses you dear cause he's always sniffing at your cap*
> *I think of all the fishing trips and all the fun we had,*
> *and when I out fished you, you never even got mad*
> *I guess you know I moved to the city, I couldn't stand being alone*
> *Because every night at four o'clock*
> *I was waiting for you to come home*
> *There were so many memories in that old place*
> *that every time I turned around I was hoping to see your face*
> *I see you every night watching the hockey games*
> *and I really believe, this year Bill,*
> *that Montreal will take the Flames*
> *Your family all misses you, we talk about you a lot,*

and after everyone is gone, Fergie is all I've got
I'll always remember you sweetheart, no matter what I do
Cause I know for one thing Bill,
there will never be anybody else but you
I love you sweet heart and miss you

5b) What are you most ashamed of?

"I'm ashamed of a lot of things I might have done, but I think one thing (in particular). When I had my children, I had a bad pregnancy and the baby was born dead. Well, she was alive for two hours, but she was a complete mongoloid baby. So, about a year later I got pregnant again and my pregnancy started out the same. And, my husband was so mad at me for getting pregnant. Well, it was his fault too. But anyway, I had to have a legal abortion. And, when I told my mom I was going to have one – it had to be approved by a psychiatrist and four doctors, and I was about four months pregnant – Mom told me that when I died I would be burning in hell for the rest of my life because I took this child away. Anyway, I never tried to go to church again or communion because she was such a strong Catholic. She said, 'Don't try to put your tongue out for communion because it will fall on the floor.' I was brought up with so much fear with religion. And, I was ashamed of having that abortion, but the doctor said the baby never would have been normal."

6) What makes you sad?

"Well I hate ... I watch Doctor Phil and all the problems people have. And, I go back to my own life as a child. I had a brother. He molested all four girls but 'you couldn't tell Mom' – you couldn't do that. I wish we would have reported him then, but it doesn't bother me now."

7) What is the hardest thing you have ever experienced?

"I think it was Mom and Dad fightin'. He would tie her up. I mean, with myself I don't know what I'd say is my hardest. I mean, when Mom died, or Dad died, or my Husband died, then Ben died, I mean, you get used to it. A lot of people here that I've met have died. You know? It's what life's all about. Well, I'll tell you that when I was pregnant that one time when I had that legal abortion. I'd go to bed at night and my husband had all these guns hangin' on the wall. Two or three times I would have gladly got up – or I had thought, because he was wild about it. I would have the books lined up on the table for the kids before school and he would get up and just wipe them all off. I was just so weak. I said to my oldest boy, 'I just can't go on like this, I just can't.' I was going to, I had my mind made up, I was going to take the two youngest kids with me – I had worked at a hotel and they had a nice creek there – I was going to take them down there and was going to do away with them and myself. The other three could look after themselves. But, then one of the neighbors called the doctor and told him he'd better come see me."

8) What is great about you?

"I think that I get along with people well. I'm very friendly. I just like myself – I do. I try to keep myself neat. I like telling jokes. And, when I got this friend of mine here you'd be surprised the things some of them said. 'Well you're not just playing Crib. You're not just doing this or that.'

I said 'What gave you the first clue?'

But, the guy is ninety (years old). What can you do? I just really like myself. I looked into the mirror this morning and said, 'Gosh darn you're not bad lookin.'"

9) Who are you?

"Well I'm not Anne Murray. Although, one time I was visiting a lady in the hospital and one lady was in the next bed and had a curtain around her. She asked me if I was a relative of Anne Murray. I said, 'No why?' She said that I sounded just like her."

10) What question do you want me to ask you now?

"I don't know. If I was down in the dumps I could probably tell you something, but when you enjoy life what is there to say?"

My time with stranger 50 was like sorting through a treasure chest. She offered piles of gold upon gold and sparkling gems of adversity and triumph. What fascinated me is how she looked at her life and spoke about her life, as if observing the experiences rather than staying attached to them. Some of her stories had me wincing in compassionate pain as she revealed the details and struggles throughout her life. She, on the other hand, looked back on all of them as fond distant memories that were all a part of creating the person she is now. She had the wisdom and perspective that time provides. Perspective: a great skill that seems to come with age. It is the ability to view your life as an intricate canal system that led you to the place you live in now.

Near the end of our time together, Stranger 50 leaned toward me and asked, "I believe that things happen for a reason, don't you?"

I thought for a while before responding. "I believe that events steer us in one direction or another," I replied.

She leaned back into her chair nodding in agreement before talking aloud about the sequence of events in her life that brought her to where she is now.

There is something interesting about the concept "happening for a reason." When we are hit hard by tragedy, or other unexpected events, we so quickly jump to the place of reason and try to make sense out of what happened. What is the significance of this? Why did this happen to us? To me? We get caught in the game of reason, coming up with every answer available to us. We can rationally understand some events, but the rationalization often leaves us conflicted and the tragedy still burns a hole inside of us. Why is this? We try and make sense of events and tragedies and attempt to escape from the emotions that scream inside of us. Why does sadness need a reason? Why does grief require qualification? What about the feeling of love? Can you make sense of that? Do you ever, after a night of passionate star gazing with the love of your life, sit down and think to yourself, why me? Would you pause before collecting a winning lottery ticket to deliberate on what you did to deserve it? No, you'd just enjoy it.

Laugh, cry, live, and love with what shows up without trying to make sense out of it. We cannot create reason from emotion. Reason and perspective come with the vision and hindsight of experience. Experiencing what arrives allows you to look back and find wisdom. Be with emotion when it arrives because emotion is energy in motion that will allow you to move forward in your life. Stop carrying the weight of old baggage and reason. Let time reveal the intricate pieces of the puzzle and heal the wounds that reason cannot.

STRANGER 51

**"...I want to know
if you can sit with pain
mine or your own
without moving to hide it
or fade it
or fix it..."**
- Oriah Mountain Dreamer

Ring...Ring...Ring... He looked at the caller ID and didn't recognize the number. He was going to let it go to the answering machine but something told him to pick up.

It has been a while since I felt this nervous approaching a Stranger. I was nervous because I was temporarily blind. I couldn't see who it would be. As the year long experiment came close to its end, I thought about the ways it would really stretch me when it came to approaching a Stranger. Walking up to random individuals had become quite easy for me, so I was searching for something different and challenging. I figured that it would take an extraordinary effort on my part to convince someone to open up over the phone by cold calling random houses and making my pitch to a faceless voice. Would I be able to build trust and rapport over the phone after interrupting someone at home? This definitely felt like a stretch for me.

My heart pounded as I stared down at the white pages about to pick a random number to cold-call. My finger sat on top of a tiny name in the "A" section of the phone book as I paused. I had a little pep talk with myself about being ok with rejection. It*'s nothing personal*, I told myself, as I stared at the cold cordless phone as if it was a weapon I didn't know how to use.

Part of my fear was that I didn't know how long this process could take before someone would agree to the interview. The story I had made up in my head was that I would have to go through each letter in the entire phone book a few times until someone would bite. It could take hours! Well, a walk of a thousand miles begins with the first step. I took a deep breathe, lifted my finger, and dialed the first number in the A section. Number disconnected.

Exhale.

Next pick: another A.

This time it rang…

Oh No! Someone picked up…

A female voice answered.

What do I say?

I made my pitch.

She must have known I was a newbie at the cold calling thing as she pleasantly told me she was unavailable and wished me luck.

This isn't so bad. Let's try letter B! It rang several times before the voice of an older man picked up. "Hello, this is Ben!" the cheery voice said. I jumped into my pitch with more confidence and excitement and then I was interrupted.

"I can't come to the phone right now. Please leave your name."

Great. The answering machine got me. I must become smarter. My skills will become strong through adversity. Let's try another B. 4th attempt. *Of how many more*, I wonder…

A deep, mature male voice quickly answered. He sounded kind and relaxed. I made my pitch.

"Sure, why not."

Really? It was that easy? My fourth cold call and someone already agreed?

Stranger 51 is a retired Baby Boomer who worked as a heavy machine operator, who pleasantly took my call to make a random connection.

1) What is your dream job?

"Oh my gosh! That is a question and a half. It would be to guide people. A motivating, comforting person that can be there when you need them with the proper advice they need. More of the sincerity that comes with 'I'd like to help you, I'd like to show you the way, or give you some guidance that will lead you the way.' Help – I'm providing help."

2) What fulfills you?

"My family. Being in contact – being close. Getting the hugs without being asked for. You know, things like that. As far as family goes, what really thrills me is just to be there for them, to know that they know that I love them, and that they're aware of that."

3) What is your greatest fear?

"Not being accepted. That's been all my life. Ever since I was a little kid I always strived for acceptance, sometimes to my own detriment. Obviously, the rejection. When you need somebody, they're not there. You know? Or when you want to talk to somebody and they don't have the time for you. No one wants to be alone."

4) What do you want more of in life?

"Peace – and not necessarily for me. I know when you say your prayers and things like that it's always for peace on earth. Well, you know what, that is a strong driving force. I'd love to see peace on earth. Unfortunately, being a realist, I know that won't happen. It's funny, my wife and I were talking about this on the weekend. What would bring more peace would be more tolerance, more consideration of others, and all of the nouns that surround that."

5a) What is your greatest accomplishment?

"For a guy who didn't finish high school as such... Well, I did afterwards. I'm from the Boomer age so I saw all the hippy stuff and was involved in some and kept away from some that was kind of dangerous. For some reason I seemed to be drawn to that kind of thing when I was younger... Personally, it's my two kids. My wife and my two kids. I don't want to leave out my wife because without her I wouldn't have my two kids. They're the greatest accomplishment in my life. I am so proud of what they have done."

5b) What are you most ashamed of?

"That I didn't succeed further in business. And, some personal things that I'd really like not to answer that. Had I some things to do over again, of course, I'm sure we'd all have done differently: causing my parents grief, causing my wife grief, causing my kids grief."

6) What makes you sad?

"Other people's pain because there's nothing that I can do to help them at that particular moment. With friends and family, I let them know I'm there. I never try to intrude on their loneliness or sadness. It's 'Hey look. If you need somebody just to be there, just to listen, or just to be beside you.' My brother did this to me once when he was going through a tough time with his wife. All he wanted was someone to listen, not someone to pass judgment or give advice or anything – just 'shut up and listen' and I did. Afterwards he said, 'that was the best thing you ever could have done for me.'"

7) What is the hardest thing you have ever experienced?

"That's tough to answer that one – really tough. I would say the death of either or both of my parents. Realizing that person that I will never really be able to talk to them. I will never be able to tell them that I love them, and I should have told them. You know? You regret. Maybe I did even tell my dad, I believe the night before, but maybe not showing it – not displaying the love and care when I had the opportunity. And, once it's gone you can never get it back. I'm going to give you a second one and that was when I put my mom in a nursing home. She wanted so bad to stay in her house until she passed away but it got to the point where it was dangerous. She had a bit of dementia. (She would do) things like leaving the stove on, things like buttering the muffin bag. She was buttering the muffin on the front of the bag rather than the... (actual muffin). It was difficult watching her lose her faculties."

8) What is great about you?

"Well, I'll tell you what I think is great about me is my capacity for caring and my capacity for compassion – for feeling what that other person is feeling."

9) Who are you?

"A loving father. A loving husband. That's the best explanation I could give you, and that's what I aspire to be."

Last weekend I spent three days observing, volunteering, and participating in a workshop that was all about the process: being in the moment with those feelings that we have a hard time being with, being with pain, being with failure, inadequacy, even forcing ourselves to be in a place of self celebration – achievement, and being with whatever is here inside of you right now. The workshop finished on Sunday evening and Monday brought an unexpected practicum.

Early in the morning, my phone rang. It was a friend who was going through tough times recently. I finished the meeting I was in as quickly as possible and called my friend back. For the next hour, I simply listened. I listened to the crying, the fear, the pain and fought the urge as much as possible to try and fix it. All I did was just listen. There were long stretches where the space was filled only with the sorrowful tears separated by deep inhaling gasps. I kept listening until it was time for my friend to go.

After this, I had begun my cold call experiment to see if someone would agree to be interviewed on the phone by me. I was absolutely shocked when the fourth attempt was a yes. I realistically thought I would go through each letter in the phonebook a few times before finally finding someone. I guess, after a year of proving myself wrong, I still don't give people enough credit. The interesting thing here was what Stranger 51 spoke about when he referred to being with other people's pain: "Just shut up and listen."

After I finished with Stranger 51, I was transcribing the audio and my phone rang again. Another friend. This one I wasn't expecting. My friend quickly shared that a mentor of his was found in critical condition and was currently on life support. They didn't think he was going to make it. My friend cried with sorrow and fear of the unknown. What next?

Ok, the universe has sent me a message. All weekend was about being with 'what is hard to be with'. What am I supposed to be learning here?

I think it was a real opportunity to just listen – to be in the place of holding the space for them to experience whatever they needed to experience without fixing, or diverting attention, or making them escape because of my level of discomfort. I was never uncomfortable, but what I have to grapple with is how I love to talk and share what I do know. And I really do think the things I have to say make an impact, but it doesn't matter. Impact or not, people don't want wisdom. They want permission to feel. They want you to be there and witness their experience – not your experience of their experience. People want to be with the pain and sorrow and expression of tears because it is not natural to keep them in. They want you to assure them it is ok to be in pain, not by telling them about how to get out of it but by being with them.

Like what someone once told me, "What we resist persists."

If we drag people away from their true experience they never get to unshackle themselves from the grief, the grief persists. My lesson in all of this? It doesn't matter how many books I read, how many experiences I have, or how good I may think I am at fixing things. My greatest asset as a friend is my presence. No words, no solutions offered, just my presence. I have to trust the whole time that their process can be and must be experienced by them.

STRANGER 52

"The final mystery is oneself."
- Oscar Wilde

He climbs. He falls. He climbs. He falls. Sometimes he doesn't know what he climbs for but he continues anyhow. There are moments when he falls when he wants to remain there, face buried in the mud, so that no one can recognize him. As he lies there a voice stirs inside of him, "Fall seven times rise eight."

The venue was a familiar one. My yoga room was a small space that held a few yoga mats, a large mirror, a massage table, and a stereo. The laminate floor was slightly warmer than the cool cement beneath it, and the dimmed lights created an orange haze around the room.

I sat and stared at a familiar face. A face I have known for many years but still have so many questions about. A face that I share numerous memories and experiences with, but many are incomplete or misunderstood. A face that, while similar, has definitely changed over the years and my childhood memories recall something different. This is someone who I am supposed to know best, but I have, many times in the past, pushed them away for the sake of others. This should be the one who has been the beneficiary of many questions from me, for all the time we spent together. But the reality is, more often than not, this person has been a recipient of assumptions. This person has been a stranger to me at times and I only find it fitting that I finish the 52 People experiment with the most important stranger in my life.

1) What is your dream job?

"My dream vocation is what I'm doing: working with people to stretch themselves beyond what they thought was possible, to become adventurers and explorers of themselves and their lives. My dream vocation allows me to express and allows me to be free to create more space for doing important things other than making money. Making my dream bigger would be expanding my impact and reaching more people."

2) What fulfills you?

"What fulfills me is meaningful conversation and relationships, when the 'fakeness' is lifted between people and authentic conversation takes place. It fulfills me when I can reveal my fear to my wife and she accepts me for the person I am. It fulfills me and humbles me deeply when friends or strangers open up and let me in to catch a glimpse of what their true life is like. What also fulfills me is the unbridled experience of full expression. singing in the shower, dancing wildly, or letting the tears run down my face when something deeply inspires me – all of this – fulfills me."

3) What is your greatest fear?

"My greatest fear greatly depends on my state of emotion. There are times when I feel like I could handle anything. There are times when the smallest thing gets blown up in my mind and the fear creeps in. But, mostly I would say I fear 'the dark'. What I mean when I say 'darkness' is many things. I fear the darkness of blind reaction – what happens in the heat of the moment when people's rage, ego, and hatred control their actions. I fear the destructive capabilities of humankind when individuals fall into this darkness. There is also a deep fear, aside from darkness, and that is not being accepted. I love to be loved, and a great fear of mine is that people will turn their back on me for some reason or other. Friends, family, colleagues... abandonment. Being left alone to fend for myself. I consider myself a pack animal who thrives while working and creating with others, so to be abandoned by others, to be rejected, is a great fear."

4) What do you want more of in life?

"I want more silence, stillness, and idleness – most of this in the context of my mind. It is easy for me to get caught up in the speed of life – getting through things to get to the next thing. When I forget to stay present in the moment, my days, weeks, and months fly past me and I remember little detail, only the fragments of memories."

5a) What is your greatest accomplishment?

"This is a tough one. I would consider my greatest accomplishment my relationship with my wife and my relationship with myself. My wife and I almost never made it. We had this great relationship that lacked something. We were the consummate happy couple who never experienced emotion. Even if we did, we kept it locked up so tightly for fear that the other should ever find out. We already possessed some of the contributors to marital collapse even before we were married: communicating based on assumptions, the belief you could actually 'win' an argument, and the belief that emotions were for the weak. After a short split-up – in which we broke down these beliefs and started over to building a real relationship – we started to grow. We learned how to cry in front of each other, show emotions openly, communicating through assumptions, and learned how to argue. Although we have made major breakthroughs, we are still working away. The way we deal with each other and love each other is so much deeper now than I could have ever imagined. A love that's real yet still challenging."

5b) What are you most ashamed of?

"There is nothing in my past that can jolt me awake at night like something that happened when I was about 13 or 14 years old. There was a boy around town named Garth. He was from a very poor family and was not very social at all. He often wore the same clothes to school the whole week, wore thick glasses which had been taped several times over, and often carried a grimy pungent odor. He rarely spoke and often made animal like noises when confronted socially. Well, one day rumor spread around the school that Garth was going to fight someone in front of his house. So, when the bell rang to end the day, hundreds of kids walked along the streets to wait in front of his house in order to get front row seats for the ensuing bloodshed. A large circle formed out front of the house. But, there was something missing: Garth. His competitor – a much more popular kid just looking to add a notch of infamy to his resume – stood in the centre of the circle punching the air in preparation, much to the delight of the raucous crowd. Far away, off in the distance, Garth was peddling his rusty BMX bike towards home. The crowd started to cheer as he got closer. Once he took notice of the crowd gathering in front of his house, he slowed down in wonderment of the number of people standing on his property. Clearly he had not heard the rumor involving himself fighting another person. He quickly peddled up and dropped his bike and attempted to run inside his house. A group of people grabbed him and threw him into the

middle of the circle and the crowd erupted with joy. He made a high
pitched growling noise as tears started running down his face, while his
competitor approached him and started swinging – landing punches to
Garth's abdomen and face. His glasses broke in two and he fell into a fetal
position crying and screaming on the ground. All the while the crowd
cheered with delight as the same people who had prevented him from
escaping into his house picked him up to resume the fight. Even while I
write this now, my stomach burns and tears build up in my eyes. The
cruelty of adolescence. Why am I so ashamed of this? Why does it still
haunt me? Well, because I was a coward. Even as the event was building,
prior to Garth's arrival, I knew it was wrong. My heart sank as he
materialized in the distance with his bike, and my heart tore apart as he was
forced unknowingly to fight someone for the shear pleasure of bloodthirsty
spectators. My heart had told me to stop it. What was happening wasn't
right! Yet, I couldn't muster up the courage to stand in front of my peers
and stop it. This is what I am most ashamed of. Knowing something is not
right and not having the courage to intervene and make it stop, it still
haunts me."

6) What makes you sad?

"What makes me sad more than anything else is to see people
treated poorly. Much like the experience of my past that included Garth,
nothing pains me more than to see people bullied or mistreated. I feel a
deep pain when I see kids, who are not as socially accepted, being taken
advantage of by others, or mocked, or mistreated in anyway. This makes
me extremely sad but also vigilant."

7) What is the hardest thing you have ever experienced?

"This is a tough question because I really think the hardest thing I
have ever experienced is myself: the way my mind has paralyzed me,
harshly judged me, and created horrible experiences for me. I have been a
master of making things so much worse than they actually are. The mental
movies I have created for myself in the past have been absolutely
excruciating at times. My hardest battles are the ones created in my mind.
So, when I say the hardest thing I have ever experienced is myself, it's
about making things worse than they really are. But, if I were to pick a

'thing' it would probably have to be being thirteen years old. Puberty, girls, competition, hormones, the cruelty of adolescence – this was hard."

8) What is great about you?

"There are so many great things about me that I'm learning to appreciate more and more every day. Some great things about me are my ability to really connect with people – make them feel comfortable and develop meaningful conversation. Also, my desire to make life better for people is something that is great about me. I'm an idealist. A dreamer – which I think is great. I also think that me expressing my emotions in an open way is something that's great about me. My ability to speak and inspire, to get people excited. I am a great husband and friend. What is great about me is that I want to become better at the things I know."

9) Who are you?

"I'll explain myself in many ways. First, I am a wolf that thrives on running with the pack. Engaging the hunt, in the chase with my team, absolutely thrills me. Wandering freely with my pack in discovering new territory, knowing the support of the pack is behind me, with me, allows me to be strong and achieve great things. I am also someone who is fighting the great battle of my ego: the pulls of greed, boredom, fear, gluttony."

I sat in my yoga room and stared back at my own reflection in the mirror. I have thought about these questions for the last year while I have been doing the experiment but have never really answered all of them. I wanted it to be as authentic as possible, not crafted. In the moment, I came up with my answers – at least my answers at that moment. Who knows what my answers would be today? Things change at every moment. What is important is that I even surprised myself somewhat with some of my own answers.

We consider those we don't know as strangers, but there is a question that hangs above us: "How well do we know ourselves?" What if I'm living inside the skin of a stranger?

It is interesting for me to look back and think about times when I was very curious about others, asking question after question, while never asking myself the same questions. How well can I really know someone if I don't know myself? It is a difficult question, I know, because it seems like the more I learn about myself the more questions I have; I realize more and more that I don't really know myself at all or as soon as I think I do I surprise myself.

I think we naturally learn to seek answers externally at a very young age. Mom knows, Dad knows, big brother knows, teacher knows – if I ask them, they'll tell me. And, so goes the foundation of the strong pattern we develop that prevents us from really turning inward to our own natural wisdom and seeking answers from within. It is here, I believe, that we develop distance between our true self and our strange self. We are conditioned to think that others "know better", so the questions stop. Or, if we do ask, we generally don't give ourselves credit – we choose not to believe our own answers. We continue to live the lives that others want us to while enhancing the distance between our true self and the stranger we live with. The distance can become so far that it takes a lifetime to reconnect. The outside has been the source of information for so long that the final mystery indeed is oneself.

The first stranger that we need to open up to is ourselves. We need to ask ourselves the right questions, allow the true answers to emerge, and connect with the most meaningful relationship in our lives: my relationship with me and yours with you.

CONCLUSION

Crusade for Meaningful Connection

One year and 52 strangers later, I have a bounty of incredible connections and reflections. My connections took place over dinner, conversations over coffee, in bathrooms, movie theaters, airports, taxis, karaoke bars, kitchens, fast-food restaurants, hotels, crowded streets, bus stops, beaches, street corners, video stores, pool decks in Florida, film-screenings, dance class, water slides, bookstores, at fundraisers, while walking on fire, in rubber dinghy's, in city parks, ice cream shops, The Castro in San Francisco, at an NFL game in Atlanta, at a gas station, hockey rink, zoo, casino, shopping mall, senior's complex, and a cold-call. Not a bad cross section.

The experiment that began on my birthday was possibly the greatest gift I could have imagined giving myself. The purpose and intention to connect with strangers had me excited about life, curious about the lives of others, and inspired by the knowledge and opportunity to share it.

At first, my intention was to spend the conclusion analyzing the answers people gave me. How many people want more money? How many people fear death? But, I feel as though the number of answers in a specific category is not the great finding. The gem lies far behind the answers and more in the space created by the meaningful connections that took place. The questions were a great starting point. They weren't too invasive, they didn't push people away, and they provided people an opportunity to reflect on certain things in their life. Where this experiment failed is that I limited myself to some extent by not exploring each individual further. While it may be a failure in regards to the limitations I gave myself, I think it illustrates the ease of creating stronger connection with others and still leaves the opportunity for more ongoing exploration as the relationships evolve.

One question that crossed my mind while engaged in this experiment was that around the sustainability of relationships. I don't believe any relationships are sustainable on their own. How well can you really know someone? Only as much as you continue to connect with them through meaningful, curious intention. People change as their experiences shape them, like the wind cuts through stone and water wears down the river banks. You can eventually peel down the layers to experience the realness between two people.

How well you know someone in this moment will undoubtedly change. The people I connected with during this experience have all but vanished now and may have different fears, dreams, and experiences. The key to sustaining great relationships is to continue the exploration and to understand that the process is on-going, not a once done destination. We do not know who the people in our lives are today. We think we know who they were yesterday and we tend to use that knowledge to create unrealistic expectations based on the experiences of the past and the problematic belief that they will remain that way. Who are they today? What makes them jump out of bed today might make them cringe in sorrow tomorrow. People are ever changing beings that will flower in front of us if given the opportunity. Sustainable relationships rely on the constancy of meaningful connection - not the simple kind of connection social media offers.

There were some myths at the beginning of the year that I set out to disprove – myths that people would tell me before I began this experiment. After a year, I feel I have enough information to either prove or debunk the myths around creating meaningful connection.

Myth #1- Connection with others is difficult - It takes too much time.

Although my body was exploding with butterflies at the beginning, it wasn't difficult at all. People were willing to take the time to sit down with me. For the most part, the connections only took between five and fifteen minutes. Some of them lasted close to two hours. It was ridiculously easy.

Myth #2- People will think I'm weird by approaching them to connect.

Some people acted as if they might be in the process of getting "punked," but for the most part people seemed genuinely willing to participate. They may have felt weird at the beginning of the interview, but for the most part they felt great at the end of it.

Myth #3- Most people will reject me.

This is one that I was fully prepared to accept at the beginning of this whole thing. This was what I thought would be my biggest challenge. The biggest learning for me, in regards to this point, is to let go of expectations. I would say that I experienced less than 10 rejections during the whole year. The stories that I made up in my mind about engaging with strangers portrayed it as if I would be swimming with the sharks. In reality, it ended up being completely different. What I thought were shark fins were actually dolphins.

Myth #4 - People will not be open with me.

There were a few strangers who didn't go too far in regards to the depth of their answers, but I was shocked at their overall willingness to dive far beneath the surface and share their deepest secrets with me. If someone didn't go very far beneath the surface, it was probably because I wasn't willing to go there. This is a huge piece of accountability for me. When I show up as someone willing to go there, I can lead others to create meaningful connection with me. They will only go where I am willing to go myself.

Myth #5 - People do not want to connect, they want to be left alone.

This is, in my opinion, the furthest thing from the truth. People yearn for connection, and I think that's a big reason why this experience was so successful. People want it so bad but don't know how or where to start.

Myth #6- People have enough meaningful connection already in their lives.

No way. I was shocked early on when I received a comment from a woman who said she couldn't imagine answering these questions in front of her husband. I couldn't believe my ears when she said it. These are the relationships that are supposed to be closest to us. If we cannot be open and share our true selves with our partners in life, who can we share them with? This confirmed to me once again that we are spending our lives living with strangers.

One of the culprits preventing connection is that people rarely listen. We often get into situations where our conversations are simply competitions against those we are speaking to – every answer you give is often responded to by the other person with a comment to match or exceed your statement. But, to be truly heard, from a curious participant, is something people really appreciate. People want to go to the scary, deep, exciting, and real places. What they need is someone to lead them there and then sit and listen without competing or turning and making it about themselves. They want someone to just listen and be curious and witness the unfolding of their thoughts.

I was so grateful to witness the depth and energy of those who spoke about their experiences – many of which they have never shared with anyone before. This confirmed something to me. It was confirmed, when I received the many hugs and heartfelt handshakes from strangers after the interviews, that going to these emotional places builds connection. Speaking about these things creates resonance, trust, and meaning with those participating. Just like our greatest failures can help shape us into wise and experienced successes – when we share these difficult thoughts, feelings, and dreams with others, it also shapes and strengthens our relationships and our learning. I found that by engaging with strangers and asking questions, I not only learned about them, but about myself and my life. Alas! I have found the secret to a meaningful life and it comes through meaningful connection. Connecting with people is a necessity for me to experience life fully. The year after the completion of the project was extremely difficult for me. It took me a long time to realize that the thing missing in my life was that I had stopped actively seeking meaningful connection with others and subsequently had become disconnected from myself and my life.

We best learn about ourselves through others, through the reflection that is in front of us. So many times throughout this experiment, the strangers that arrived in my life taught me lessons or created reflections that were important for me. We are creatures of community and must embrace and expand ourselves within the community to fully realize our ability to grow. I have felt this deep inside of me before, and this experiment has simply confirmed that.

So this is the bottom line: STOP LIVING WITH STRANGERS!

My relationships continue to change and I strive to do my part to make those changes. I work to no longer rely on the weather, sports, economy, housing market, television, or anything else to be the foundation of my relationships. I have realized and accepted that the foundation of all my relationships is me – who I show up as and what I bring.

Our time on this planet is limited. We know this yet we let our relationships slip through our fingers and allow ourselves to live with people we don't really know. We will grieve hard when people die, and the regret will burn deep inside. You can continue on this path, or you can change. There is something you can do right now to create more meaningful connection in your life: GET REAL WITH THE PEOPLE CLOSEST TO YOU.

Approach someone and tell them how important they are to you, ask them about their illness, or what they're greatest fear is – this opens the door to developing something with meaning. Talking about your truth and exposing your vulnerabilities are the ingredients for greatness in relationship. It does take trust, but that is built quickly through action. You may get hurt at some point in the process, but I'm certain you will recover and begin again. This is life. I will take the pain of rejection any day rather than carry the regret of an unfulfilled relationship.

Relationships are everything. They create meaning to otherwise dull moments, they make great experiences even greater, and when you look back on your life you will remember the people you touched and those who touched you. You will relish those moments when you experience the exponential product that arises when two people lean into one another. This is life. The depth of your life will be measured by the depth of your relationships.

From the moment we are born we have a gift that we all possess in equal sums – the gift to reach out and connect with anybody, anytime. The richness of life awaits you. Connect with complete strangers. Connect with acquaintances, and, most importantly connect with the strangers that are closest to you.

The end of Dallas' life was the beginning of great learning and the birth of a great movement. As this experiment ends, it also forms a new beginning. Now a great shift begins and it depends greatly on you.

AFTERWORD

Six Degrees of Separation

It was a warm November day, almost a year after completing 52 people. I was driving down the highway when my cell phone began to ring. I glanced down at the screen and it indicated that my wife was trying to reach me. I picked up.

"Yello?" I playfully shouted.

"I'm so sorry," she immediately pleaded, deviating from our normal ritual of phone greetings.

"What? What are you talking about?"

"I gave your number to someone I probably shouldn't have."

"Who?"

"Mitch Stevens."

My mind instantly drifted back 13 years to high school when I met the scrawny quiet kid who claimed he had a desire to play football. The head football coach at the time introduced us and asked me to keep an eye on him. I was a returning senior and he was a grade ten kid. Initially, I looked at him and figured Mitch would have no chance in football but figured I'd help my coach out and look after him.

I invited Mitch out with us one afternoon and after a short while we struck up a friendship. He quickly could be found either hanging out at my place playing video games or lifting weights with me. We shared our past with each other, like friends do. I soon found out Mitch had experienced a much different life growing up than I had.

His mother struggled with alcohol and drugs, and his step father was abusive. Mitch had run away one night, at the age of eight years old, and spent the cool night in a downtown city park amongst the homeless and drug dealers. He was quickly scooped up by social services and began bouncing around different foster homes over the years. During those years, he would display frequent rages of anger that led him to spending time in a secure boys' home. After a while of staying out of trouble, he was reintegrated to foster care and began public high school.

254

As years passed, Mitch and I had become close friends and training partners. After high school we kept in touch. I watched proudly as he grew into a mountain of a man and began dominating the football league. We connected briefly on the same team playing junior football, but I ended up moving to bobsleigh and he wound up moving east to further his football career. Our interactions became less than those of a friendship. And, soon enough the phone calls I was getting were not from the motivated training partner and friend looking for advice on how to get stronger or faster. He called me many nights – intoxicated on drugs, alcohol, or both – frequently asking me for money. Mitch always had a story about how someone *"screwed him"* and he just needed a bit to get him through. I gave in a few times but began to screen my calls. They kept coming, but I stopped answering. Every time I resisted to temptation to pick it up and hoped he'd get the message to stop calling. Erin knew all about him and was aware of my previous attempts to stop communicating with him. It had been close to three years since my caller ID had displayed his name.

My wife sat apologetically on the other line as she explained how she thought it was a coaching client trying to reach me.

"Sweetheart don't sweat it. There's nothing we can do about it now," I assured her. "I will just have to change my number," I joked with her, before hanging up.

It was no longer than a minute before my phone rang again. I cautiously picked it up. "This is Jayson."

"Jayson, this is Mitch Stevens, how are you?"

We continued to make small talk for a while, asking about each other's jobs and families, before I sensed some nervousness in Mitch's voice.

"What's up man? You sound nervous," I said.

"I have a confession to make. I stumbled across your 52 People experiment on Facebook and fell in love with it right away. I couldn't stop reading it and when I got to Stranger 4 my head almost exploded."

I quickly thought back to Lenny, the homeless man who became Stranger number 4.

"I have a confession to make," he repeated nervously. "I'm the guy who kicked his head like a football and almost killed him."

All of the muscle strength in my jaw instantly vanished as my mouth gaped wide open in disbelief. Like a great blue whale scooping up plankton, my mouth remained motionless as my mind tried to put a million pieces of the puzzle together in that brief moment.

"I'm sorry," he said. "After I read your blog I told my girlfriend and I called my Mom and just had to share this with them."

He continued to tell me about the whole story.

After evading police for a few days he was tracked down by police, found guilty of assault, and spent time in jail. While in jail, he laid awake many nights contemplating his future. Mitch remembers asking himself if he wanted to continue living the life of a criminal or if he was willing to do what it took to change. When he was released from jail, he moved out to the east coast where he met a great girl, got a job, and now has a small child of his own.

"Mitch, I'm so grateful that you'd call to share it with me," I expressed.

"I had to get it off my chest. And, if you can use this at all, go right ahead. Let others know that people make big mistakes, but they can change."

We continued speaking for quite some time until I slightly changed the subject. "Hey Mitch, do you mind if I ask you ten questions?"

ABOUT THE AUTHOR

Jayson Krause, CPCC, is a former three time national champion in the sport of bobsled, a coach, speaker and leadership consultant. He is the co-founder and CEO of Driven By Passion Inc., an international business designed to inspire connection. Jayson currently live in Okotoks, Alberta with his wife and children. To learn more about Jayson and his keynotes, coaching and seminars, visit www.drivenbypassion.com